THE GARDENER'S BIRD BOOK

THE GARDENER'S BIRD BOOK

A Guide to Identifying, Understanding and Attracting Garden Birds

by Tom Carpenter

NATIONAL HOME
GARDENING CLUB

National Home Gardening Club

Minnetonka, Minnesota

About the Author

Every month of the year finds
Tom Carpenter finding plenty of
excuses to get out where the
birds are—both near and far
from home. When he's not out
with them, he's watching
goldfinches, cardinals, woodpeckers, nuthatches, blue jays,
hummingbirds, grosbeaks,
buntings, warblers, native sparrows, redpolls, pheasants (and
more) from the windows of his
Minnesota home. This is his third book on nature and the outdoors, and
his writing has also been featured in a variety of national magazines.

The Gardener's Bird Book

6 7 8 9 / 06 05 04 03

ISBN 1-58159-054-7

National Home Gardening Club
12301 Whitewater Drive
Minnetonka, MN 55343
www.gardeningclub.com

Tom Carpenter
Creative Director

Michele Teigen
Senior Book Development Coordinator

Gina Germ
Photo Editor

Patricia Bickner Linder
Book Design and Production

PHOTO CREDITS

Francis C. Berquist pp. cover, 5, 6, 9, 11, 16
both, 17, 18, 27, 30, 31 both, 37, 38, 49, 50, 56 (2),
57, 60, 62-63, 64, 86 both, 87, 92, 96, 100, 103,
104, 106, 107, 127, 133, 149, 156, 158 both, 160,
166, 174, 175, 176, 189, 197, 198, 199, 205; **Don
Enger/Animals, Animals** pp. cover, 3, 20, 171;
Donald M. Jones pp. cover, 18, 21 both, 27, 54,
68, 69, 75, 87(2), 99, 105, 127, 130, 132, 139, 148,
166, 167, 197, 203; **Bill Marchel** pp. cover, 6, 10
both, 11, 15, 45, 55, 67(2), 70, 71, 73, 76, 82(2),
83, 90, 91, 93(2), 98, 129, 131, 145, 146, 156, 160,
166, 168-169, 170, 172, 182, 190, 191, 192 both,
193 both, 196, 199, 204(3), 205; **Maslowski
Photo** pp. cover, 6, 7, 14-15, 19, 22 both, 23, 24,
28, 32, 33, 36, 37, 38, 39, 42 both, 43, 44, 48, 51,
52, 53, 54, 56, 57, 61, 63, 65, 66, 70, 72, 78, 79,
80(2), 84, 85, 88, 93, 95(2), 97, 100(2), 101, 102,
118, 122, 123, 124(2), 125, 132, 133, 134, 143,
144, 148, 150, 152(2), 153, 162, 164(2), 165 both,
175, 176, 184, 185, 186 all, 187, 191, 200, 201,
202(2), 205; **Richard Day/Daybreak Imagery**
pp. 6, 7, 8-9, 11(2), 44, 48, 49, 55, 65, 66, 74, 79,
80, 81, 84(2), 90, 98, 102, 106, 128 both, 129, 130,
138-139, 142 both, 144, 146, 150, 164, 170, 172,
173, 178, 182, 184, 185, 196, 198, 200, 202; **Greg
Berquist** pp. 5, 26, 34 both, 35 both, 43, 46 both,
47, 51, 57, 68, 74, 87, 89, 92, 131, 197, 204, 155,
160, 169; **Brian Milne/Animals, Animals** p. 20;
George Godfrey/Animals, Animals p. 24;
Arthur Morris/Birds As Art pp. 26, 29 both, 32,
43, 45, 72, 73, 88, 98, 108-109, 109, 110, 111, 112,
113, 114, 115, 117, 119, 121, 122(3), 123(3), 124,
125(3), 134, 135 both, 147, 154-155, 161, 162,
171, 181, 190, 198, 204, 205; **G.W.
Willis/Animals, Animals** p. 33; **TC
Nature/Animals, Animals** pp. 58 both, 59;
Todd Fink/Daybreak Imagery pp. 60, 61, 104,
124; **Cliff Beittel** pp. 76, 120, 151, 157, 159, 163,
205; **John Gerlach/Animals, Animals** p. 76;
David Boyle/Animals, Animals p. 107; **Bob
and Ann Simpson** p. 116; **George Bryce/
Animals, Animals** p. 163; **Donna Ikenberry/
Animals, Animals** p. 177; **Jack Wilburn/
Animals, Animals** p. 177; **Fred Whitehead/
Animals, Animals** pp. 180-181; **Robert
Lubeck/Animals, Animals** p. 182; **Jeff
Milton/Daybreak Imagery** p. 183;
DenverBryan.com p. 189; **Patti Murray/
Animals, Animals** p. 188; **Paul Berquist/
Animals, Animals** p. 188; **Bill Holister** pp.
194(2), 195 both; **Wildlife Forever** p. 194;
Roger Aitkenhead/Animals, Animals p. 196;
Robert Maier/Animals, Animals p. 197; **Susan
Day/Daybreak Imagery** pp. 1-2, 200; **Robert
McKemie/Daybreak Imagery** p. 103, 205.

Contents

CHAPTER 1

Finches

CHAPTER 2

Chickadees, Nuthatches, Wrens & More

CHAPTER 3

Thrushes & Other Large Songbirds

CHAPTER 4
Warblers

CHAPTER 5
Woodpeckers

CHAPTER 6
Native Sparrows

CHAPTER 7
Swallows & Flycatchers

CHAPTER 8
Hummingbirds

CHAPTER 9
Gamebirds & Waterfowl

Introduction

Welcome to The Gardener's Bird Book. *It's like three bird-lover's volumes all rolled into one!*

As gardeners and bird lovers, there just never seems to be one book that balances all our interests.

To start, there are field guides to help us identify the birds that visit our yards and gardens, and the birds we are fortunate enough to spot when we're out on a walk or even in field or forest bird watching. These guides are detailed (sometimes almost to a fault), but they get their job done well: When you've finished looking at the photos and/or drawings, and reading detailed descriptions of various birds' looks, there's often little doubt. You have narrowed the potential field and positively identified the bird.

But field guides leave a little something to be desired. Sure, they help you know what you're looking at, but you get few to no details about understanding that bird—discovering what really makes it tick. Does it eat seeds or insects? Prefer heavy cover or wide open spaces? Stay near water or keep its feet on dry ground? Nest in bushes, trees,

Important planting decisions go beyond trees and shrubs. What goes into the ground, grows, flowers and seeds this year can also help the birds—in various ways, at various stages of its life. Here, a pair of black-capped chickadees feeds on a sunflower seed head in autumn. The ideas in this book will help you steer your decisions to keep birds in mind.

tree cavities or on the forest floor? These facts behind the bird and its life strategy are important. Knowing the details—the bird's history and living strategies—is inherently interesting, much moreso than just knowing the common and Latin name of what you're looking at.

Finally, once you have identified what has been visiting and then figure out some of the details about its secret life, it would be nice to get some real-life advice on attracting that bird to your yard and garden on a more regular basis. No doubt there are some good books in this respect too, but they don't always get specific about the bird at hand, and about the habitat you can create and the offerings (seeds, water and otherwise) that will work to bring in that particular bird.

Sometimes the best action you can take is no action at all. Cut down any trees with a little rot and a few holes in them, and you'll destroy important nesting habitat for a bird like this house wren. You'd also be getting rid of a prime feeding tree for woodpeckers. Better to "leave it up" as long as you can—and let nature's beautiful visitors make up for any lack of perfection it brings to your garden. Ideas like this abound in this book.

When making planting decisions, keep the birds in mind. Many substitutes could have been made for this crabapple, but this Bohemian waxwing would never have visited had there not been fruit to harvest. Create your landscape with an eye and attitude toward attracting the birds you like, or want to see more of; this book makes plenty of suggestions.

The Gardener's Bird Book *offers three simple premises (hence, it's* **A Guide to Identifying, Understanding and Attracting Garden Birds).**

This book rolls all three topics into one concise package.

The first idea is this: Bird identification is simple if you have a good, representative picture and a few clear, concise and focused notes to go on. The second idea: When you get to read about the everyday habits and survival strategies of that bird, you gain a real understanding of how he goes about life. Finally, you'll find specific, real techniques for making sure your garden habitat, and the foods and other things you offer, are geared to that bird.

Hummingbirds are the garden's smallest—but in many ways its most exciting—bird visitors. This rufous hummingbird is feeding on sugar water. We'll teach you about making and serving that, but you'll also discover important strategies for making your garden habitat friendly to hummingbirds. An important factor here is what you plant, and we've included many plant lists, including one linked to your region of the country.

Unconventional ways of making offerings are often the most interesting. Here, suet was forced into holes bored into a piece of log. The look is natural; the birds love the presentation too. In this book, you'll discover a variety of other unconventional (but effective) ways of making offerings.

What you offer the birds isn't restricted to the staples of seeds and water. This northern oriole is a confirmed fruit eater—he would never really come to seeds of any type—so this orange half serves as a perfect attractor. Plus, the bird (and possibly his nestlings) gets some good nutrition. Besides this and other fruit, other non-seed food offerings you'll read about include suet (animal fat), grubs and insects, jelly, even sugar water.

How The Gardener's Bird Book *works.*

*Y*ou've probably never seen a bird book like this, and that was our idea in creating it!

Start out with the bird's common name and Latin name. Then read about the species' history, habits and habitat in a small, easy-to-read but detailed essay on the subject. Special tips for identifying, understanding and attracting that species of bird are included; many of these tips have photographs included, to illustrate points.

You get a detailed range map with summer (yellow), winter (blue) and year-round (green) ranges indicated.

There are also detailed identification notes, as well as highlights on all the bird's nesting strategies.

RANGE MAP
YELLOW = SUMMER RANGE
BLUE = WINTER RANGE
GREEN = YEAR-ROUND RANGE

COMMON NAME

LATIN NAME

DETAILED ESSAY

TIPS FOR IDENTIFYING, UNDERSTANDING AND ATTRACTING THE BIRD

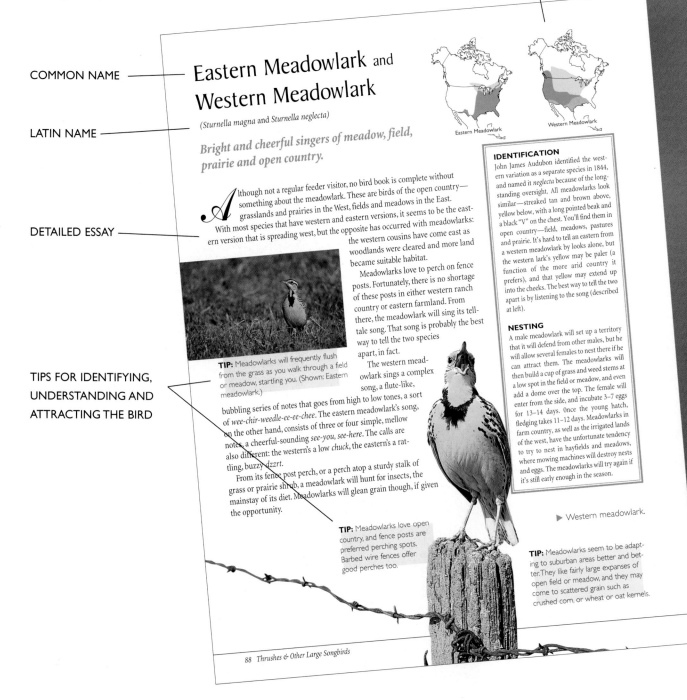

Eastern Meadowlark and Western Meadowlark

(Sturnella magna and Sturnella neglecta)

Bright and cheerful singers of meadow, field, prairie and open country.

Eastern Meadowlark   Western Meadowlark

*A*lthough not a regular feeder visitor, no bird book is complete without something about the meadowlark. These are birds of the open country—grasslands and prairies in the West, fields and meadows in the East. With most species that have western and eastern versions, it seems to be the eastern version that is spreading west, but the opposite has occurred with meadowlarks: the western cousins have come east as woodlands were cleared and more land became suitable habitat.

Meadowlarks love to perch on fence posts. Fortunately, there is no shortage of these posts in either western ranch country or eastern farmland. From there, the meadowlark will sing its tell-tale song. That song is probably the best way to tell the two species apart, in fact.

The western meadowlark sings a complex song, a flute-like, bubbling series of notes that goes from high to low tones, a sort of *wee-chir-weedle-ee-ee-chee*. The eastern meadowlark's song, on the other hand, consists of three or four simple, mellow notes, a cheerful-sounding *see-you, see-here*. The calls are also different: the western's a low *chuck*, the eastern's a rattling, buzzy *dzzrt*.

From its fence post perch, or a perch atop a sturdy stalk of grass or prairie shrub, a meadowlark will hunt for insects, the mainstay of its diet. Meadowlarks will glean grain though, if given the opportunity.

TIP: Meadowlarks will frequently flush from the grass as you walk through a field or meadow, startling you. (Shown: Eastern meadowlark.)

TIP: Meadowlarks love open country, and fence posts are preferred perching spots. Barbed wire fences offer good perches too.

IDENTIFICATION

John James Audubon identified the western variation as a separate species in 1844, and named it *neglecta* because of the long-standing oversight. All meadowlarks look similar—streaked tan and brown above, yellow below, with a long pointed beak and a black "V" on the chest. You'll find them in open country—field, meadows, pastures and prairie. It's hard to tell an eastern from a western meadowlark by looks alone, but the western lark's yellow may be paler (a function of the more arid country it prefers), and that yellow may extend up into the cheeks. The best way to tell the two apart is by listening to the song (described at left).

NESTING

A male meadowlark will set up a territory that it will defend from other males, but he will allow several females to nest there if he can attract them. The meadowlarks will then build a cup of grass and weed stems at a low spot in the field or meadow, and even add a dome over the top. The female will enter from the side, and incubate 3–7 eggs for 13–14 days. Once the young hatch, fledging takes 11–12 days. Meadowlarks in farm country, as well as the irrigated lands of the west, have the unfortunate tendency to try to nest in hayfields and meadows, where mowing machines will destroy nests and eggs. The meadowlarks will try again if it's still early enough in the season.

▶ Western meadowlark.

TIP: Meadowlarks seem to be adapting to suburban areas better and better. They like fairly large expanses of open field or meadow, and they may come to scattered grain such as crushed corn, or wheat or oat kernels.

Make this book your one-stop bird reference and resource.

FULL PHOTO
(USUALLY OF THE MALE)

Knowing the right seeds to offer, and which type of feeders to put them in for various species of birds, can spell the difference between success and failure in attracting specific birds to a feeding station. These goldfinches definitely find niger thistle in a tube feeder to their liking. You'll find many more good feeding ideas and guidelines on the pages that follow.

Finally, and certainly most beautifully, your eyes will drink in a full-page photograph of that bird in all its glory, often with inset photos to help you identify females of that particular species or members of a related subspecies.

Of course, there are other types of pages in this book as well, including our bird galleries. The galleries don't go to quite the level of detail shown here, but offer good overviews on a variety of members of a particular bird family.

Creating a book like this isn't easy. Thousands of photographs get whittled down to the best of the very best. Tens of thousands of words get worked and re-worked into a concise, readable, accurate package. Pages and pages of designs get fine-tuned into beautiful, flowing packages made to please the eye and present all the information attractively, concisely and logically.

But it's all for a purpose, and a very good one at that: To provide you with the absolute best gardener's bird book you will ever see. To that end, we hope we have achieved our goals. You are the judge now. Enjoy *The Gardener's Bird Book*, and all the birds of your yard and garden!

MAY ALSO INCLUDE AN INSET PHOTO
(USUALLY OF FEMALE IF MALE AND FEMALE DIFFER IN LOOKS)

Finches

From a goldfinch's neon yellow to a cardinal's royal red, the finches bring a spectrum of color and bundles of energy to the garden. Even the less-spectacular finches—like the active pine siskin, elegant purple finch and lovely rose-breasted grosbeak—will make your heart sing when they visit. The members of this family are among the easiest to plant for and attract, because for the most part they are seed eaters. They are also easy to identify because they vary so much in color, size and habits.

A garden with finches is a garden full of joy.

American Goldfinch

Carduelis tristis

A gaudy and handsome bundle of joy that brings neon-yellow flashes of life to grasslands, gardens and backyards.

To know the American goldfinch is to know joy on wings. A summer male—with his bright, canary-yellow plumage punctuated by a handsome black cap and wings—provides a feast for the eyes, to be sure. But in her own right, so does a female in her more reserved but delicate and attractive plumage of olive, gray and dusty yellow.

Goldfinches are seed eaters, period, which explains why the birds nest so late in the year. They wait for mid- and late-summer's abundance of weed seeds before even thinking about pairing off and then working together to build a nest in a shrub or sapling. There, they will feed their babies "goldfinch porridge"—partially-digested seeds they bring back to the nest.

And seeds are what the goldfinch is about. Day-in and day-out, his survival depends on seeds, and the most important of these is thistle. But tree seeds, seeds from weeds tall and short, sunflower and other flower seeds, even the seeds from vegetables that have bolted … all are fair game to the opportunistic goldfinch. A flock can really brighten a day, fluttering in to a feeder or patch of dried flowers, hanging every which way to extract seeds, and then all of a sudden they are gone, off to find another cache of seeds.

Goldfinches are the perfect backyard and garden bird (see tips) because they prefer relatively open country such as the meadows, prairie and other open areas with an "edge" component of shrubs or trees. Listen for the telltale calls—a *chew-chew-chew* triplet when in their roller-coaster flight, or a happy *per-chick-oree* call when feeding.

TIP: Goldfinches are fairly easy to attract. One of the best ways is to hang a tube or other feeder and keep it filled with niger thistle seed. Goldfinches also love black-oil sunflower, whether in the hull or out.

TIP: Providing the right type of nesting cover—deciduous shrubs and small trees—could bring nesting goldfinches to your yard.

IDENTIFICATION

At 4½ to 5 inches in length, the goldfinch is smaller than a sparrow. You can't miss the male's bright yellow plumage (from April or so to September), black cap and wings. Females, young and winter males are gray/olive, often with hints of yellow, with black wings and white wing bars. Look for the birds' scooping, roller-coaster flight and listen for the calls described. As with other finches, the goldfinch can sing beautifully as well, and the male does his warbling tune at breeding time.

NESTING

The goldfinch weaves a wonderfully sturdy cup of grass from late June to September, often lining it with the down of thistle, milkweed or other plant down. Some nests are so tight they can hold water. The 4 or 5 pale blue eggs hatch in 12–14 days and the young fledge about 16 days after that. Unlike many other songbirds, which feed their young insects, male and female goldfinches feed their young a partially-digested blend of seeds.

TIP: Goldfinches love a bath and a drink, so a simple birdbath is a wonderful way to get the birds visiting your garden or yard.

TIP: Plant some sunflowers and leave them up for winter goldfinches. It's also important to leave some wild, grassy "edge" around your yard if possible; this female goldfinch is perched atop a thistle.

Pine Siskin

Carduelis pinus

This cold-weather visitor from the North warms birders' hearts with high-energy activity at the feeder.

To have a flock of pine siskins visit your yard is to see energy in action—hustling, bustling, aggressive little birds jockeying for their turn at a feeder. No matter where you live, you're most likely to see pine siskins in the depths of winter or, possibly, just either side of it. Why? Because these are true boreal birds of the Arctic, venturing south into the U.S. only when their seed supply is short in their homeland.

In that sense, the pine siskin is a lot like the goldfinch, and the two are closely related. Pine siskins seem to focus more on tree seeds though: pine, hemlock, spruce, cedar, elm, alder, willow and others ... probably reflecting the far northern habitat they prefer.

Although at first pine siskins appear to be just another brownish-looking bird at the feeder, you'll notice some subtle but handsome features such as the delicately-streaked breast, and yellow patches on the tail as well as the bases of the wings. A small, pointed beak also separates the siskin from larger-beaked sparrows.

Of course, having some pines around helps—siskins just seem to feel at home around them, surely a reflection of the boreal forest they have to occasionally leave in search of food. Even their Latin species name is *pinus*. From late fall to early spring, you can see a pine siskin most anywhere in our country ... and roamers they are. If you get a visit, enjoy them right then because tomorrow or the next day they may be gone on another nomadic journey in search of seeds.

TIP: The pine siskin's name is no coincidence: The birds love pines and other conifers, for the cover and nesting sites available, as well as food in the form of seeds.

IDENTIFICATION

Pine siskins are small, at 4½ to 5 inches in length. To make a positive identification, look for a streaked belly and small yellow patches within the tail and on the wings. Still don't know for sure? Look for a notched tail. Pine siskins also have a small, pointed beak, the better for extracting the conifer and other tree seeds they love. Listen for the *bzzzzzzzzt* call, and a song like a raspy-sore-throated goldfinch.

NESTING

The pine siskin creates a shallow nest of moss and twigs, from April to July, and lines it with plant down. The nest is usually in a conifer of some type. In the U.S., the Mountain West sees some pine siskin nesting activities, in conifer forests where high altitude replicates the boreal conditions of the Far North. Three to 4 spotted, green-blue eggs hatch in 13 days with the young fledging about 26 days after that.

TIP: To identify a pine siskin, look for a streaked breast, yellow patches on wings and tail, and a distinctive forked tail.

TIP: Niger thistle is the best way to attract pine siskins to a feeding station. Their beaks are perfectly suited to digging the small seed out of a thistle-feeder port or thistle sack.

In addition to thistle, siskins will come to sunflower, millet, even suet. They seem to prefer their sunflowers hulled. Pine siskins also love to pick up salt off roadways, a trait common to all the northern finches.

Common Redpoll

Carduelis flammea

A handsome visitor from the Arctic, where he is a sacred symbol to ancient religions of the land.

The Cree and Inuit people of the Far North hold the redpoll in reverence in both legend and religion, and for good reason: The redpoll is the only small song-bird—and the only bird period, save the ptarmigan—that regularly spends its winter in the Arctic. The natives' respect for this tiny bird is borne out of that fact … inspiration from a bird that also makes its year-round home in such a harsh, unforgiving land.

TIP: The redpoll is a winter visitor, irrupting into the U.S. when its favorite food—seeds—is in short supply in the Arctic.

But just as the people of those northern tribes are resourceful, so is the redpoll. When times are really tough in the Arctic—for the redpoll, a failed seed crop in the birch, willow and tamarack brush it calls home—flocks head south into the U.S. and that's when we see them. These *irruptions* (mass, temporary migrations) can thrust as far south as Texas, Alabama, Georgia and South Carolina, but more often the birds find what they're looking for—seeds—in the northernmost tier of states.

When they do come, redpolls descend upon any type of seed they can find; weedy fields and roadsides, birch and alder trees, and feeders (see tips) are favorite places. Visits from redpolls are special, and if you get some coming to your feeder, enjoy them; you might not see them again for three, four or five winters.

But when they do come, they are beautiful indeed—from their red caps and black chins to their delicate gray striping to the telltale washes of rosy-pink on the breast and flanks. Don't expect just one or two birds—they'll come in a swarm of boundless energy and infinite good cheer to brighten a winter day.

IDENTIFICATION

A redpoll is a tiny (5 to 5½ inches in length) but stylish package. On the male, look for the red cap and the gorgeous brushstrokes of rosy-pink on the breast. Females will feature a very deep red cap, almost black sometimes, and a markedly black chin. Both sexes are grayish brown on the back, with soft striping. Also look for the forked tail, typical of the small finches, and listen for their songs—a rattling trill or a hoarse *swee-ee-ee* sound similar to the goldfinch's.

NESTING

Redpolls nest in the Far North, creating a tight little cup of moss, twigs and grass, and then depositing 5–6 tiny, pale green eggs in the down-lined nest. Incubation takes 10–11 days and the young fledge a dozen days after that. Successful parents may try to raise a second brood in the April–August breeding season.

TIP: There is a closely related red-poll, the hoary redpoll *(Carduelis hornemanni)* that is in some ways even more striking than its "common" cousin. The difference: the hoary red-poll looks "frostier" with a lovely, paler breast and an unstreaked rump; it is also slightly larger.

TIP: The best way to get redpolls to stop in your yard: Hang a thistle feeder of any kind. Redpoll beaks are well suited to the tiny seeds. Also, once the birds come, try spreading thistle, sunflower chips, peanut hearts or other seeds on the ground to serve the crowds because chances are there won't be enough feeding ports on one or even a couple feeders.

Northern Cardinal

Cardinalis cardinalis

Our most familiar red bird, anything but ordinary with its striking, crested beauty.

Here is one songbird species that has truly benefited from human settlement of the land. It started as the saw and then the plow cut into our country's vast and mature eastern forests, creating the openings that offered the brushy edges cardinals love. More and better habitat meant more cardinals, and the birds' range expanded. In fact, cardinals used to be more migratory, with northern birds heading to the southern states for the winter, where they joined resident birds. Now, good habitat and bird feeding keep many birds in the North year-round.

And what a sight a male cardinal is—in the winter especially but at any other time of year as well—with his deep red plumage, handsome crest, black face and red bill. But a female cardinal displays a classy look all her own, dressed in her crested suit of browns, grays and creams, with hints of rosy red on the wings and tail; she has a red bill.

Cardinals are seed eaters, and it's easier to list the types of seeds they won't eat than the types they will. But in summer, when there's a nest of hungry youngsters to feed, insects will comprise up to 50% of the diet. Cardinals do much of their feeding on the ground or near it, hopping and flitting around while making their sharp *chip* calls.

Cardinals are easy to please (see tips) because they love seeds and they love a patch of brush they can call their own. They are often the first bird to a feeder in the morning and the last one to leave in the evening—almost at dark—to help you start your day with a capital letter and end it with an exclamation point of beauty.

TIP: You can get cardinals to visit a tube feeder, if you attach a seed tray for them to perch on.

TIP: Cardinals love black-oil sunflower seed. The seed is best placed on a stationary or platform feeder, as the cardinal likes solid footing. Here, a courting male feeds a female.

TIP: Plant evergreens—such as Black Hills spruce, arborvitae, cedars and others—to provide the security cover and nesting habitat cardinals need.

IDENTIFICATION

Cardinals measure 8 to 9 inches in length, and you can't miss the male's royal-looking, red plumage. (The birds were named after the color of the robes of Catholic cardinals.) Look for the male's black face. Females are more subdued but no less beautiful with their rosy-red-washed plumage of brown, gray and cream. Listen for the cardinal's beautiful song—often *what-cheer, what-cheer, what-cheer, whit-whit-whit-whit*. Songs vary widely though, and different regions' cardinals will sing different songs. What's consistent is the clear and beautiful tones. Locate cardinals in the brush by the *chip* calls they make.

NESTING

Cardinals get busy early in the spring, in hopes of raising a second brood after the first batch fledges from a nest built of twigs, leaves, rootlets, tree bark and plant fibers. The nests are almost always placed fairly low (10 feet or lower) in dense shrubbery or a thicket, often in a young evergreen. It's rare to find a cardinal nest because they're usually so well hidden! In preparation for breeding duties, the male becomes kind and gentle, even feeding the female at the feeder during courtship and then as she incubates. The pair works together to feed and raise the young.

▶ Inset: Female cardinal.

Purple Finch

Carpodacus purpureus

An elegant-looking finch dressed in wine-colored feathers, heading for a party in the pines.

The purple finch is an attractive bird, to be sure, with the male looking as though he took a bath in a puddle of red wine. Roger Tory Peterson described the purple finch wonderfully by saying it looks like "a sparrow dipped in raspberry juice," and that's a perfect description too.

But there's even more to love about the purple finch than just its good looks.

TIP: Purple finches will eat almost any kind of seed, but they prefer sunflower at the feeder. They're not picky as to what type of feeder they visit, and will go to a platform or a hanging tube; they're used to working hard for the seeds they get.

First is the song—a rich, fast and lively warble. If you have pines, spruces, cedars or other fairly mature conifers around, you may be fortunate enough to have purple finches nest there and serenade you with their songs. More likely though, unless you live in the Far Northern U.S. states, you'll see the purple finch during migration times—the bird simply shifts north and south a bit with the seasons—and in winter at the feeder.

That's the other endearing trait about the purple finch. Primarily a seed eater, the bird is fairly easy to attract to feeders (see tip), and the purple finch loves natural seeds such as ash, birch, box elder, cedar and spruce. In season, they'll take fruit such as mulberries, raspberries and wild grapes.

Purple finches tend to hang together in flocks, and in summer they seem to prefer wilder woodlands—usually coniferous ones—over suburban parks and yards. But as the weather gets colder in fall, as winter drags on and as spring seems like it's finally coming, look for purple finches in your yard and at your feeder.

TIP: Any grouping of conifers—pines, fir, spruces, hemlocks or cedars—provides good purple finch cover. The birds will also find food there: the seeds in the cones.

▶ A female purple finch. Notice the light-colored stripe over the eye, and streaking on the breast.

IDENTIFICATION

On the male, look for the soft wine or raspberry color on the head and upper breast (fading to cream and gray the lower you go), and rump. Compared to the house finch, the purple finch is lighter and more elegantly colored overall, and lacks streaking on the breast. A female purple finch is brown and gray, with a distinctive white stripe over each eye, and a delicately streaked breast; these traits distinguish her from a female house finch. Both male and female purple finches measure 5½ to 6½ inches in length.

NESTING

A purple finch heads to coniferous woods in breeding season, creating a cup of grasses and twigs and lining it with hair and other soft materials. This nest may be as high as 60 feet off the ground, often at the end of a long limb. There, the female lays 4–5 bluish green, brown-spotted eggs. The young hatch in 12–13 days, and fledge 2 weeks after that.

House Finch

Carpodacus mexicanus

This native of the West is adapting to life in cities and suburbs of the East, Midwest and South.

The house finch presents many interesting contrasts. He is a native of the American West, particularly the Southwest, hence the species name *mexicanus*. (Another common name for house finch in that region is *linnet*.) Yet the house finch resides in much of our country at present. How? Birds were brought to New York City for sale as cage birds in the 1940s. When that was outlawed, pet store owners released the evidence—the birds. The hardy finches adapted well to city and suburban life, and have been expanding their range eastward and southward ever since.

That presents some pluses and minuses. On the plus side, the house finch is an attractive bird with his shoulders, upper chest and face of red, orange, yellow or some combination thereof. And the bird sings a beautiful song—a cheery warble that certainly brings joy to many an urban or suburban street, or backyard. And house finches are willing visitors to feeders too, but therein lies one of the minuses.

Aggressive birds, house finches easily outcompete native birds, such as goldfinches and chickadees, at the feeder. House finches also travel in fairly large groups of 6 to 10 birds, further complicating matters as they monopolize a feeding station and chase the smaller, gentler guests away.

So make your own judgment on the house finch. He provides a lot of happiness for bird lovers who might not otherwise have songbirds around. But he can be a brute, an outsider taking over much-needed territory from birds you might prefer.

IDENTIFICATION

The male sports a red, orange or yellow face, bib and rump, to some degree; the actual color is a result of the bird's diet. The female is drab brown, with a streaked breast, but she lacks the facial stripes or white eyebrow-streak of a female purple finch. The house finch is sparrow-sized (5 to 6 inches in length) and sings a nice song, which varies with regions and individual birds; the voice is a little raspier than the purple finch's.

NESTING

House finches are opportunistic nesters. They have built nests in forgotten Christmas wreaths near front doors, in bird houses and in hanging flower baskets; they also utilize shrubs of all kinds. The nest is usually well made, woven of grass, and the female lays 4 or 5 lightly-spotted, pale blue eggs there. The youngsters hatch after 13 days of incubation by the female, and fledge 14 days after that.

▶ Inset: A female house finch lacks the white stripe over the eye that is characteristic of the female purple finch.

TIP: One way to discourage house finches from hitting all your feeders is to provide some tube feeders with the feeding ports *below* rather than above the feeding perches. House finches have weak feet, and won't be able to feed here; this will allow chickadees, goldfinches, nuthatches, siskins and other smaller natives to have a spot of their own.

TIP: House finches will come to most any type of bird feeder and bird seed (even a stump will do), but seem to prefer black-oil sunflower. They'll also hit your thistle feeders. Be prepared—these hungry, numerous visitors will empty a feeder fast!

TIP: The house finch does sing a nice song, a redeeming quality of an otherwise aggressive bird. One small benefit is that house finches may outcompete the foreign house sparrow.

Rose-Breasted Grosbeak

Pheucticus ludovicianus

Handsome seed-eater with a bib of rosy red.

*M*ost bird lovers would be hard-pressed to name a bird more striking than a male rose-breasted grosbeak with his shiny black head, back and wings, white belly and underparts, and telltale triangle of rose-red on the breast.

But there's more to the rose-breasted grosbeak than just pleasure for the eye. Human ears love the rose-breasted grosbeak as well, listening to the bird's lilting, rich carol that is similar to a robin's, maybe even more musical. Your garden will love having rose-breasts around too, for these birds love to eat bugs, especially potato bugs. In fact, in Colorado rose-breasts are called just "potato-bug bird" because they love potato beetles so much. In the garden, grosbeaks also eat grasshoppers, cankerworms, caterpillars, moths of all kinds and beetles. Blossoms and buds are also in the diet.

Rose-breasted grosbeaks winter in Mexico, Central America and northern South America, so the time of year to enjoy them in the U.S. is in the spring and summer. When they're here, a rose-breast's diet consist of about 50% animal matter (chiefly insects like those mentioned above), and 50% seeds, fruits and other plant matter. Those foods are what the bird's massive bill is all about—cracking the seeds and crunching the insects.

You can attract rose-breasted grosbeaks to your yard (see tips), especially during the spring migration. If you want them around all summer long, you'll have the most success if the right habitat surrounds you or you create it—mature trees and plenty of brush and shrubs, for this grosbeak is a forest bird. They seem to especially prefer riverbottoms and creekbottoms, which is where they seem to appear first each year—rose-bibbed greeters singing beautifully from the treetops.

TIP: A rose-breasted grosbeak at the feeder is a pure delight. Black-oil sunflower on a tray feeder, or hanging tube feeder with a tray, will bring in birds.

TIP: Rose-breasted grosbeaks love fruit—barberry, elderberry, mulberry, raspberry and much more—and eat them seeds-and-all. Even a cherry pit isn't too tough for that powerful beak to crack. The types of shrubs these fruits grow on also provide good cover for grosbeaks.

IDENTIFICATION

Males and females are about 7½ inches long, and are very similar to a cardinal in profile and general size, if you omit the crest. A mature male is handsome and unmistakable in his coat of black and white, set off by the gorgeous, triangular rose-colored bib. A female is much less conspicuous with her heavily-streaked plumage of brown. A prominent white eyebrow distinguishes her from other brown birds of similar size, as do the extra-large grosbeak bill and yellow wing lining (if you see the bird in flight). An immature male looks a lot like a female, but he has a pink-washed breast. The song is crisp and rich, similar to a robin's. At the feeder or from foraging birds you'll hear single, short, metallic-sounding *chink* notes.

NESTING

A pair works together to build a nest—a simple, flimsy affair of twigs, straw, grasses and rootlets, often lined with a bit of hair or other soft fibers—which they place 4 to 15 feet off the ground, low in a tree or high in a shrub. Rose-breasts often nest along the streams, rivers and other bottomlands they seem to gravitate to. The female lays 4 to 5 speckled eggs of pale green, blue or even purple; the one consistency is that the eggs are blotched, usually with brown. Both the male and female share incubation chores, and the young hatch in a dozen days, then fledge only 9–12 days after that.

▶ Inset: Female rose-breasted grosbeak.

Evening Grosbeak

Coccothraustes vespertina

Originally a citizen of Mountain West, this handsome finch now breeds to the Atlantic, and winters across our country.

No one can identify the exact reason these stocky, stunning finches have so successfully expanded their range. One theory is that an increase in winter bird feeding has allowed evening grosbeaks to spread eastward. Another scenario, equally likely, pegs the birds' expansion to the expansion of the box elder tree—a "weed" tree not especially loved by humans but relished by evening grosbeaks for the copious amounts of seeds it produces.

But the real truth doesn't matter as much as the pleasure of watching these beautiful birds and all the hustle-and-bustle they bring to the winter garden. A male, with his chocolate-brown body, yellow breast, black-and-white wings and prominent yellow eyebrow, is a sight to behold. But in her own way, a female is no less handsome in her soft washes of yellow.

Evening grosbeaks get their name from the time of day you'll often see them at the feeder, and from their gorgeous sunset colors. In fact, the Latin species name *vespertina* comes from *vespers*—evening prayers.

If you don't live in evening grosbeak breeding range, your best chance to see one is in winter. Although the birds are hardy, if local seed crops fail they will irrupt southward and that's when you can see their high-energy activity and antics. And that may be the only complaint you ever hear about having a flock of evening grosbeaks visit—there may be so many of them (up to a hundred) that you'll have a hard time keeping enough seeds coming to fill their hearty appetites.

When they're not at a feeder, almost any seed is potential fodder for an evening grosbeak: maple, ash, elderberry, spruce, fir, hackberry, juniper, Russian olive, snowberry and more. They'll also take some insects (especially spruce worms) in summer, feeding the high-protein food to their nestlings.

Though he is an itinerant visitor, this bird of the pine-studded alpine West, and of the coniferous northwoods, can bring you a sense of those places' wild beauty.

TIP: Expect a lot of guests when the grosbeaks come to dinner. But the menu is easy—black-oil sunflower seed for hors d'oeuvres, main course and dessert.

TIP: A large tray screen feeder (above) will support all your raucous guests, but most any feeder will do—even a trash can lid or piece of plywood propped up on a couple of sawhorses.

IDENTIFICATION

Look for the large, conical and very powerful-looking bill, the better to crack seeds open with; this bill will usually be pale green or yellowish in color. On the male, look for a chocolate-brown body with yellow on the lower back, rump and underparts, and a bright yellow eyebrow across the forehead. The female is less conspicuous, but still features yellow swaths on her gray plumage. Both males and females have black-and-white wings, and measure about 8 inches in length (starling-sized). Even though the Latin name *vespertina* suggests vespers or singing, the reference is apparently only to the bird's plumage and the time of day you see them, for evening grosbeaks are weak singers; usually you just hear a series of short, *chink, chirp* or *clink* notes.

NESTING

Evening grosbeaks seem to prefer conifers for nesting, building the structure high in the tree and concealing it well. Before mating and egg-laying, the male and female go through an elaborate courting, dancing ritual. The nest is just a shallow cup made of twigs and rootlets, and lined with moss, hairs and lichens. Three to 5 white to blue-green eggs, spotted and speckled with brown, hatch after 14 days of incubation by the female, and the young fledge another 2 weeks after that.

TIP: You might not like that box elder in the odd corner of your property, but the evening grosbeaks will. Just leave it go—for these, and other, seed-loving birds!

▶ Inset: Female evening grosbeak.

Blue Grosbeak

Guiraca caerulea

The South's grosbeak, a private bird of thickets and hedgerows.

The bird world is full of interesting parallels—namely, similar birds evolving to fill similar niches but in different types of habitat. The blue grosbeak is a case in point.

Although his color is a deep and handsome blue, accented by two buff-colored wing bars, note this grosbeak's typical thick, powerful beak—used on the seeds, fruits and occasional insect the bird eats. The habitat, though, is a bit different from the bird's rose-breasted and evening cousins; the blue grosbeak sticks to brushy edges, overgrown pastures, fencerows, hedgerows and other "thicket" types of places. Same foods but different places equals room for another wonderful grosbeak!

Blue grosbeaks winter in Central America, true tropical finches that return to roughly the southern half of the U.S. each year to nest and raise young. The basic summer range extends from California in the West, up to Colorado, and then across the country's midsection to New Jersey, and then south to Florida.

Listen for the blue grosbeak's nice song—a melodic warble similar to the purple finch's—and the short *klink* or *chink* call given while foraging.

TIP: The blue grosbeak is a bird of thick cover—brushy edges, tangles of shrubs and vines, and streamside thickets. Habitat like this on the margins of your yard and garden will serve blue grosbeaks and many other birds as well.

IDENTIFICATION

Male blue grosbeaks are a deep blue color, with a stout, blue-gray beak. One identification challenge is deciding whether you're looking at a blue grosbeak or an indigo bunting (see pages 36-37). Here's how to tell: A blue grosbeak's wings feature two buff-colored bars (the indigo bunting has none), and the blue grosbeak's beak is prominent and large, dominating his face. Female blue grosbeaks aren't blue at all, but rather blend in to their surroundings better with their buff-brown coloration that turns lighter as you head to the underparts; but the buff wing bars remain, although they are not quite as vibrant or rust-colored as the male's. Both males and females measure about 6 to 7 inches in length, a bit larger than a sparrow but not quite robin-sized yet.

NESTING

Look for blue grosbeak nests in shrubs, tangles of vines, thickets or even a clump of grass—a fairly casually built little bowl of grass, weed stalks and leaves. In this private hideout, the female will lay 3–4 pale blue eggs. The male is a vigorous defender of their little territory. The young hatch in about 12 days, and fledge 13–14 days after that.

▶ Inset: Female blue grosbeak.

TIP: Although not typically thought of as a feeder bird, you can sometimes lure blue grosbeaks out from cover with offerings of sunflower seeds, safflower or peanuts spread on the ground.

Pine Grosbeak

Pinicola enucleator

A tame and friendly winter visitor from the North.

*L*ife is harsh in the boreal forests that sprawl across the top tier of Canada, on up into Alaska. The pine grosbeak resides there year-round, but ventures south into the U.S., where we can enjoy his company, when seed and dried-fruit crops fail in his homeland and he has to look for new forage. Like other boreal birds, though, you will also find pine grosbeaks residing year-round in the higher elevations of the Mountain West.

No matter where you find them, pine grosbeaks are handsome birds indeed, the male with a rose-red coat, the female donning a gray cape with soft yellow twinges on the top of her head and rump.

Typical of the grosbeaks, pine grosbeaks use their powerful bill to gather and crack the seeds and fruits that sustain them both in

TIP: Pine grosbeaks will visit feeders in winter, accepting black-oil sunflower with special delight, but also taking whatever else is available. After the migration they made to get to your feeder, they aren't going to be too choosy.

summer and harsh, bitter winter cold. Pine grosbeaks will take some dried fuits, such as crabapple, viburnum or highbush cranberry, mash them for the seeds inside and then drop the pulp. They also seem to like mountain ash, hawthorn, cedar, juniper and dogwood fruits.

When life is easy and pine grosbeaks are where they want to be, they'll reside in coniferous forests across their range. In winter, when times are tougher, they'll range out farther in search of fruit trees with some freeze-dried offerings remaining on the branches, as well as tree seeds of all kinds. This is when we bird lovers can be graced by their presence—usually in a good-sized flock with at least a dozen but maybe several dozen birds. Pine grosbeaks are well-behaved guests, calm and confident, compared to some of the frenzied visitors you'll get at a winter feeder.

TIP: Dark wings with white bars, along with a dark tail, distinguish the pine grosbeak from purple finches and crossbills.

IDENTIFICATION

The pine grosbeak, at 9 to 10 inches in length, is the largest of the grosbeaks, approaching the robin in size. The male is rosy-pink or red, and distinguished from similar birds (purple finches, red and white crossbills) by his dark wings with two white bars, and his dark tail. The beak is stubbier than that of other grosbeaks, but still thick and powerful looking. A female pine grosbeak is pretty as well, exchanging the rosy-pink for predominantly gray feathers with dull yellow-green tinges on the head and rump; her wings are dark like the male's, also with two white wing bars, and she has a dark tail too. The song is a soft, musical warble, and pine grosbeaks also whistle a clear *tew-tew-tew* call.

NESTING

The farther north you go, the shorter the trees get and the closer the pine grosbeak's nest will be to the ground. The pair places it in a conifer, creating a bulky saucer out of twigs, moss and rootlets and then lining it with soft grass and lichens. The female incubates the eggs (which are pale blue in color and spotted with brown or gray) for 2 weeks, and the young fledge about 20 days after that. This is a fairly long fledging window, but remember this is the largest grosbeak—it just takes longer to get the young up to size.

TIP: *Gros* means large, and *beak* is self-explanatory. Put them together and you get *grosbeak*. Sometimes we take bird names for granted, but few are random! This particular grosbeak is almost always found in or around pines. Add *pine* to the mix and you get *pine grosbeak*. That sums things up pretty well.

▶ Inset: Female pine grosbeak.

Indigo Bunting

Passerina cyanea

Flashes of brilliant blue in woodland openings create happy feasts for the eyes.

Though the indigo bunting's species name, *cyanea*, comes from the Latin *cyan* (which is now a printer's term for blue), ink can only try to re-create the magnificent, iridescent blue of a male indigo bunting. My first encounter with these stunning birds was at a privet hedge in the backyard of my boyhood home, on the edge of town. A pair nested there for two summers, wonderful seasons that caught me watching the colorful male and attractive female by the hour, coming and going.

Indigo bunting blue was as unbelievably vibrant then as it is now, only I don't see them as often these days. No one really does, unless they're very fortunate. How was I to know how elusive these birds really are, and what a treat it is to even glimpse one?

And that's often all you'll see of the indigo bunting—a flash of blue here or there, maybe perched on a limb for a few seconds, and then he's gone—chasing the insects he loves to eat, and picking up an errant seed now and then, possibly some berries in the fall.

But when the indigo bunting is in the shadows, as he often is due to the woodland edges, thicket and brushlands he prefers, he appears almost black. It is only in the sunlight that the stunning blue is readily apparent. As you might expect with the flashy coloration, the indigo bunting is a neotropical migrant, spending the winter in South America and returning to the U.S. in the spring. Through the summer, he ranges over the eastern half of the country where his favored, dense habitat is present.

IDENTIFICATION

The male indigo bunting is just that—a brilliant, indigo-blue color, deep and rich in the sun as the bird pauses in a patch of light in a woodland opening. He is smaller (at 5 to 5½ inches long) than a blue grosbeak, with a smaller, less stout, more pointed bill, the lower half of which is white. The female is pretty in her own way, with her delicate brown coloring, pale breast, and maybe a twinge of powder blue on the wings. Listen for the distinctive call and song. The call is a single *spit* or *tick* given while foraging. The song is a series of rapid double notes sounding like *sweet-sweet, where-where, chew-chew, cheat-cheat,* but varying between individual birds.

NESTING

The female selects the nesting site low in a sapling or shrub, usually no more than 5 feet off the ground, and builds the nest—a small cup of leaves and grass, often lined with hair for softness. There she lays 3 to 4 pale blue eggs that hatch in 12–13 days. The young fledge quickly—only 8–10 days after hatching—so that the parents can go to work on a second brood. Life is tough on small, highly migratory birds like the indigo bunting, and the more young the parents produce, the better chance there will be some offspring to make the huge round trip and return next year to carry on the species.

TIP: If you have some odd, woodland or brushy corners, leave them intact. That's about all an indigo bunting asks for in order to make a stop in your yard, stay awhile, maybe even nest.

TIP: Though primarily an insect eater, the indigo bunting will take advantage of easy seed offerings—a tube thistle feeder will attract birds, as will millet or other seed spread on the ground. Keep any type of seed close to the dense, woodland kind of cover these buntings prefer.

▶ Inset: The lazuli bunting (*Passerina amoena*), a close relative of the indigo bunting, fills a similar niche in the West. In fact, the two will interbreed where their ranges overlap.

Red Crossbill and White-Winged Crossbill

(Loxia curvirostra and Loxia leucoptera)

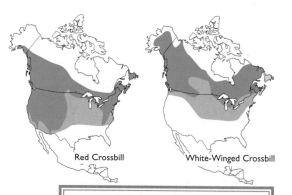

Red Crossbill   White-Winged Crossbill

It's no mistake—this handsome bird's crossed bill is perfectly adapted to a life eating conifer seeds.

There's no mistaking a crossbill when you see it. If it's your first one, you'll feel a little sorry for it before you realize what it is, what with that misshapen bill and all … it looks odd and not just a little painful. But then watch the crossbill wrestle a cone from the branches of a spruce or pine tree: He will hold the cone still with one foot and use that wonderful bill to pry the scales open while slipping a tongue in to pull out a seed. No way could this be done with a standard-order, straight bill like most birds'. No more feeling sorry for this bird!

Crossbills are nomads. This is of course true in winter, when a flock's voracious appetite might gobble up a seed supply (individual birds have been known to extract and eat over 3,000 seeds in a single day—that's how efficient that bill is). But this wandering is normal at other times of the year too, with the gregarious, nomadic flocks moving around as needed to take advantage of the seeds maturing at different times, in different places, over different species of trees.

While it's true that crossbills love pines of all kinds, spruces of all descriptions, firs and tamaracks too, these opportunists don't pass up chances to eat non-conifer seeds. They use their crossed bills to eat maple, birch, willow and other seeds as well.

Crossbills are a treat to watch, to be sure— not only for this unique feeding adaptation, but also because they're handsome. Male red crossbills sport a dusky brick-red color, and whitewings are aptly named for the two white wing bars that distinguish them from red crossbills (see identification notes for more tips). Look for them mostly in the winter, when they will venture south or head out of the mountains if seed crops are scarce.

TIP: Crossbills live mainly in pine, spruce, fir or other conifer forests, where they use their wonderful, crossed bills to pry open cones and extract seeds. This is a female red crossbill.

TIP: Crossbills are fairly easy to attract, if they're travelling through your area: black-oil sunflower seeds will draw them in for a meal. This bird is an immature male.

IDENTIFICATION

Red and white-winged crossbills look very similar, with the males of both species having a dull red overall look, accented by a black tail and wings. A male white-winged crossbill may be a bit lighter in overall coloration, but the best way to distinguish him from a red crossbill: identify the whitewing's two broad white wing bars. Females of both species are olive-green with yellow rumps, and the same dark to black wings; white-winged females sport the same wing bars as do their mates. White-winged crossbills are just a hair larger, with a full-grown bird stretching maybe to 6¾ inches; a red crossbill might be as small as 5¼ inches long. Listen for the *chip-chip-chip chee-chee-chee* song, or warbles and trills during breeding.

NESTING

Being seed eaters and concentrating on conifers at that, crossbills aren't restricted to breeding only in the spring and summer months. Seeds are available year-round, and some birds will pair off as early as January and start nesting if they find a seed-rich forest area they take a liking to. This is an extraordinary thing when you think about what the temperatures might plummet to. But whether it's January or August or anywhere in between, the nest will usually be out at the end of a conifer branch—a saucer of bark strips, plant stems and roots, lined with moss or plant down. The female incubates for 12–14 days, and the youngsters fledge 17 days after that.

▶ Shown: Male red crossbill.

Chickadees, Nuthatches, Wrens & More

Whatever some of these small birds may lack in stylish color, they more than make up for in personality and willingness to frequent your yard and garden. A visiting chickadee warms the heart with its telltale chickadee-dee-dee call, wrens will gladly fill nest houses you provide, and nuthatches will provide you with hours of acrobatic entertainment.

It would be nice to harness some of the happiness these garden visitors bring, then release it whenever needed, for whatever reason.

Black-Capped Chickadee

Parus atricapillus

Handsome, cheerful, acrobatic and entertaining, this feeder favorite warms the hearts of every bird lover.

Chickadees don't ask for much, but they offer many gifts to the appreciative viewer. A few black-oil sunflower seeds in the feeder, a little brush as security cover, a few trees in which chickadees can forage for insects, eggs and larvae—that's all you need to enjoy this wonderful and interesting feeder bird.

Why does everyone love the chickadee so much? Perhaps it's because he's a loyal friend who will be with you in all the seasons, but maybe moreso in winter when he frequently comes in from the countryside to frequent city, suburban and rural yards. Or, it could be the telltale, buzzing *chick-a-dee-dee-dee* call that lets you know a flock is coming, working and feeding its way through the tree branches. And part of this tiny bird's allure certainly has to do with his high-energy ways, including a penchant to grab a seed from the feeder—going through any and all necessary contortions and acrobatics—before flying off to a tree branch or other perch to energetically crack open the seed with his beak while holding it down with one foot.

A chickadee's diet is evenly split between animal matter (insects, eggs and larvae) and seeds. In fact, chickadees will even store some seeds for later use. Another adaptation to withstand the rigors of winter: A bird can lower his body temperature during a frigid night, to save much-needed energy before slowly awakening and going back to work the next morning. Then, chickadees will join in mixed flocks with titmice, creepers, downy woodpeckers and white-breasted nuthatches, the loose group each working their own strategy to find seeds, insects or larvae in the winter woods or backyards.

Few packages as small as the chickadee generate as much interest. The birds are relatively common, and fairly easy to attract (see tips). But birders' love for them—whether you're on a wilderness hike or watching one flit to and from the feeder as you do the dishes—is unparalleled.

TIP: Use a tube or globe feeder to dispense seeds for chickadees. You can enjoy their acrobatics, and many larger, dominating birds will shy away from the feeder. Black-oil sunflower seeds are the hands-down favorite.

TIP: Put up a nest box to attract nesting chickadees. The hole should be only 1⅛ inches in diameter. Line the box with 3 to 4 inches of wood shavings to replicate a natural hole; the birds seem to want a little work to do, removing some shavings and rearranging the rest, before calling a place home.

IDENTIFICATION

There's no mistaking the chickadee's black cap and bib, tiny black beak and bright white cheeks. The underparts are creamy white, often fringed with a twinge of buff or rust. A steely-gray back and tail round out the 5-inch-long package. Listen for the telltale, buzzing *chickadee-dee-dee* call, which helps keep the flock together as it forages through woods or yards. You'll also hear the chickadee's *fee-bee* (first note higher-pitched than the second note) song, which is actually a territorial warning. Look for the bird's incredible acrobatics as it clings, rolls, swings and creeps every which way to gather a meal.

NESTING

The chickadee is a cavity nester, and will use a natural hole created by a woodpecker or any other source, or a hole the little birds excavate themselves out of rotten wood. There the pair builds a neat cup of grass, plant down, moss and feathers, where the female lays 6–8 tiny, white, brown-spotted eggs. Both parents do incubation duty, and the eggs hatch after 12 days. The parents work like bandits to feed them (high-protein insects for the most part), and the young emerge to fledge about 16 days after that. There's nothing as cute as a tiny, fluffy chickadee coming out to see the world for the first time!

TIP: Chickadees also love to eat suet, fat and any other animal matter you place out.

▶ Top inset: A boreal chickadee wears a brown cap.

▶ Bottom inset: Mountain chickadee.

White-Breasted Nuthatch

Sitta carolinensis

This upside-down feeder creeps down tree trunks to probe the bark's crevices for insects, spiders and their eggs.

White-breasted nuthatches are citizens of the forest, and you can find the birds almost anywhere in the United States, save for a narrow strip right down the middle of the Central Plains. Most any deciduous or mixed forest will do, whether it's a huge expanse, a small wood-lot, a river- or creekbottom strip, even wooded and semi-wooded parks and yards. Nuthatches seem to prefer having a good supply of mature trees around, and I've often noted their presence around oaks in particular.

But no matter where you find him, the nuthatch offers one unique adaptation: This acrobatic bird works *down* a tree trunk or from the outer edges inward along a branch, probing the bark's cracks and crevices for the insects and spiders that hide in those breaks, as well as bug larvae and eggs.

At first this trait might seem a little common-place, but when you think about it, you have to marvel at the beauty of the strategy. Why? Because the other birds that feed amongst the bark or trunks and branches (namely woodpeckers but also creepers) work their way up the trunk or outward along the branches. The pickings might be slim for a nuthatch following the same strategy, so he goes at matters from the other, less picked-over angle. The long, slightly upcurved bill is perfect for the job.

Although insect matter dominates the diet in spring, summer and fall, seeds comprise a major component of a nuthatch's food during the winter months. You'll most often see nuthatches high in the trees, working the yards or forest with a mixed group of chickadees, nuthatches, creepers and wood-peckers. Nuthatches are great feeder birds whose acrobatics will entertain you for hours. You'll know when they're coming—listen for the distinctive, nasal *yank-yank-yank* call.

TIP: To attract nuthatches, hang a basket with a block of suet inside, then watch the birds cling and work it over.

IDENTIFICATION

A truly handsome bird, the white-breasted nuthatch is between 5 and 6 inches long. As the name implies, the breast is a creamy white, and the tail's underparts sport a wash of chestnut. The bird is a handsome blue-gray above, with a dark cap above a white face, and a beady black eye. Want to distinguish a male from a female? A male's cap is darker—tending toward black—while a female's cap is lighter in tone, bluish or dark gray depending on the region. Remember—if the bird you're watching is creeping down a tree headfirst, it's most certainly a nuthatch! As for the voice, other than the *yank-yank-yank* call, listen for the song—a series of low *whi-whi-whi-whi* notes.

NESTING

Like the chickadee, the white-breasted nuthatch is a cavity nester, building a cup of grass and twigs lined with feathers, moss, hair and other fibers in a hole. Old wood-pecker holes are favorite spots, but any cav-ity will do, and occasionally a pair of birds will excavate one themselves if the wood is soft enough. The eggs—5–6 of them, white and speckled with brown, red or gray—hatch in 12 days. The young emerge 2 weeks after that, ready to start probing on their own for insects like the ones mom and dad have busily been transporting to them.

TIP: Nuthatches love deeply-barked trees, and work them from the top down (see inset photo on next page), probing for insects, larvae and eggs.

TIP: Unlike some cavity nesters, white-breasted nuthatches are a little picky about their real estate, wanting a real tree to nest in. If you put up a nest box (opening size: 1¼ inch), try lining the outside with bark to give it nuthatch "curb appeal."

TIP: Nuthatches also love sunflower seeds, and will come to most any hanging feeder. They love to stash seeds, so don't be surprised to see birds flying off with your offerings.

Red-Breasted Nuthatch

Sitta canadensis

This nuthatch of the Northland prefers pines, even when visiting in the winter.

*I*n many ways the red-breasted nuthatch is similar to the white-breasted, and the two evolved on parallel tracks but in different regions.

As for similarities—the red-breast also creeps down tree trunks, not up them, in a never-ending search for insects, spiders and larvae. The red-breast also utilizes his bill—slightly upturned like his white-breasted cousin's—to grab these morsels. The red-breasted nuthatch eats seeds as well, although his focus—conifer seeds of all types—reflects his habitat.

That habitat is primarily the coniferous forests across Canada's bottom tier, although red-breasted nuthatches will summer along the spine of the Appalachians as well as the pine and fir forests of the Mountain West, where the elevation more closely approximates the northerly latitude of the Canadian forests.

But you don't have to travel to any of those places to see a red-breasted nuthatch. The best way is to have your feeding station set up for them (see tips) and wait for fall, winter or even earliest spring. This is when irrupting red-breasts will venture most anywhere in the United States, looking for seeds to eat to replace a failed or eaten-up crop in their normal range.

One day you'll be out on a walk in the woods or watching your feeder back at home afterward, see a nuthatch and say, "That's unlike any nuthatch I've ever seen!" Enjoy red-breasts when you can, because they may be gone tomorrow, off again in search of pines and seeds.

IDENTIFICATION

At about 4½ inches in length, the red-breasted nuthatch is noticeably smaller than a white-breasted. On the red-breasted nuthatch, look for a black cap as well as a black stripe through the eye; the rest of the face is white. The other distinguishing featuring is outlined in the name—a rusty-red breast, sometimes seeming almost orange in tone. The back is blue-gray, and the beak, though shorter than a white-breasted nuthatch's, is still pointed. The call is a high-pitched *ank-ank-ank*. Red-breasted nuthatches love pine trees and coniferous forests; that's where they're most at home.

NESTING

Here is another cavity nester. An interesting nesting habit is the pine pitch the parents often smear around the entrance to a nest hole—maybe to improve their own grip for their frequent trips in and out, possibly to discourage predators from reaching in for the downy little chicks nested in their soft-lined cup of twigs and grass. Those youngsters hatch from 5 or 6 brown- or red-spotted eggs, and then fledge in approximately 15 days.

TIP: Peanuts and sunflower seeds will bring red-breasted nuthatches in. Keep your feeders filled, as you never know when redbreasts will show up, and if there's nothing to eat there, they will move on immediately.

TIP: Red-breasted nuthatches love pine and spruce trees of all kinds—both for cover and for the seeds found there.

TIP: Most any type of suet or fat will also attract red-breasted nuthatches, eager for a high-protein meal during the lean days of winter. Try placing a bone in a mesh bag, like a potato bag, and hang it from a tree branch. Or, use a standard suet basket as shown here.

Tufted Titmouse

Parus bicolor

Much more than just a crested chickadee, this handsome, two-toned bird has an appeal all its own.

It has been said that the tufted titmouse is just a chickadee with a crest. While the two are closely related (both in the genus *Parus*), there's a lot more to love about the tufted titmouse than just its acrobatic, chickadee-like antics at the feeder.

First, the crest adds a new element to the titmouse's look—and he is the only such small songbird to have one. (A titmouse raises this crest when feeling aggressive to other birds.) Second—the titmouse has a look all its own, when you couple that crest with the blue-gray back, creamy white belly and rusty sides. Third—the titmouse's call is very different; a series or chant of notes sounding like *Peter-Peter-Peter-Peter* or *here-here-here-here*.

The habitat is similar to that of the chickadee—woodlands of all types, as well as urban and suburban backyards in winter. Tufted titmice are willing feeder visitors (see tips), and have that chickadee-family trait of flying off with a seed to hold it down with one foot while cracking it open for the meat within, before flying back for another seed.

Titmice love to eat insects and their eggs and larvae, and those foods make up about 80 to 85% of the bird's summer diet. In winter, the mix shifts more toward seeds, and only about a quarter of the total food intake then is animal matter. Titmice are often one of the birds you'll see feeding in a winter mixed-species flock, working its way through the quiet woods or the somber backyards.

TIP: The tufted titmouse is another cavity nester. Use a hole 1¼ inches in diameter on a nest box. Place a few wood shavings inside, but leave plenty of room because mom and dad titmouse like to do some decorating of their own, stuffing a seemingly impossible amount of leaves, moss, bark, hair, fibers, plant down and other material in there.

TIP: Simply enough, black-oil sunflower will attract titmice in winter, when they are concentrating on seeds more than animal matter in their diet.

Suet is a good offering for titmice too. A titmouse is an insect eater at heart, and it's hard for the birds to pass up that high-calorie animal matter as an extra "boost" to the day's feeding.

IDENTIFICATION

The tufted titmouse measures about 6 inches long—sparrow-sized but more slender, and just about an inch longer than a chickadee. Look for a steely-gray bird with a white belly and rusty-tinged flanks. The feet seem quite large (the better for clinging every-which-way off branches and twigs to glean insect meals), and the black beak is tiny. Don't know for sure? Look for the crest; even when it's not being displayed, you will be able to see its longer feathers, dropping off the back of the bird's head. If the crest is displayed, there's no mistaking it. In Texas, where the tufted titmouse sports a black cap, it was until recently thought to be a different species.

NESTING

The male and female will stuff a hole or small tree cavity with leaves and moss, where the female will deposit 5 or 6 creamy white, brown-spotted eggs that only she will incubate—usually for 13–14 days. The young fledge 17–18 days after that. Titmice know that times can get tough, so they usually will attempt to raise a second brood, if the first one comes off well. If they are successful with that second brood, the young from the first brood will sometimes participate in feeding the new chicks. Family groups may stay together throughout the winter.

▶ Inset: In the West, the plain titmouse replaces the tufted titmouse. Plain titmice seem to especially like habitat with oak brush.

Dark-Eyed Junco

Junco hyemalis

Once thought to be four separate species, four variations on this wonderful bird frequent winter feeding stations across the country.

For such a simple, friendly and successful bird, the junco has seen a hotbed of conflict. That conflict started when early ornithologists started identifying different subspecies of junco, based on plumage variations found in different regions and habitats.

There was the slate-colored junco, which was most widespread and loved, typically the bird of the East and North, right over to the northern Rockies. Then you had the western or Oregon junco, a similar bird but with brownish sides. In the central Rockies, you might find the pink-sided junco (a self-explanatory name), and in the southern Rockies you could see a gray-headed junco, discernible because of the orange-red patch on its back. In the Black Hills of South Dakota and Wyoming, you would find white-winged juncos.

But all this junco jockeying proved fruitless, because it was discovered that the birds readily interbred where their ranges overlapped; that overlapping is very common, being that the junco is a very migratory bird, especially in winter. That's when you're most likely to see juncos— when they come down from the mountains or the Far North, in search of seeds for winter food. Juncos are birds of the ground, and love forests, brushy edges and other treed areas.

So now we have one junco—the dark-eyed junco—and many delightful variations. While juncos aren't stunning birds, they are still handsome in their coats of slate-gray, bellies of white, and twinges of brown or orange or rust depending on where you are. One of the interesting things about juncos is that, although they are fairly nondescript, there are very subtle variations even within a flock of birds at, say, a single feeding station. Take some time to study and enjoy the individual differences.

TIP: Predominantly ground feeders, juncos will pick up most any seed spilled from other feeders. You can also make special offerings for juncos, because they need it: Spread white proso millet, cracked corn, black-oil sunflower seeds, bread crumbs, even grain. When hungry enough, the birds will feed at your hanging and platform feeders as well. Shown: an Oregon junco.

TIP: Juncos are winter visitors, and almost all feeder surveys identify them as our most common winter guest. They'll come in late fall, stay for the winter, then leave in early spring. They hang together in roaming flocks, sometimes as many as 20 birds, at this time of year.

IDENTIFICATION

The junco is sparrow-sized, at about 6 inches in length. As discussed, there are many variations on the bird. In general, look for the slate gray back, white belly with a very sharp distinction between the white and gray, a beady black eye, and a pink or yellowish bill. One common trait is the white outer tail feathers every bird features—a telltale sign you are looking at a junco. You'll see these feathers flash as the bird takes flight, probably a signal to other birds in the flock that something may be awry, it's time to move on. Listen for the song—a long, ringing trill. Juncos also make high-pitched *clink* and *tick-tick* calls and twitters while feeding.

NESTING

A pair of juncos builds a deep, sturdy cup of grass stalks, rootlets, moss and strips of bark; this nest is usually placed on the ground, or concealed under vegetation, a blow-down tree, a brushpile or even an overhanging bank of dirt. There the female lays 4 or 5 gray-green, brown-spotted eggs that hatch in 11–12 days. The young fledge 12–13 days after that. Nesting takes place in the far northern reaches of junco range, predominantly in the boreal forests of Canada. Resident birds in the Rockies and Appalachians take to secluded, high-altitude forests to do their nesting duties.

▶ Shown: Western form of the junco.

▶ Inset: Northern junco.

Brown Creeper

Certhia americana

Seldom seen, this mouse-sized bird is actually very common, creeping up tree trunks in forested areas.

*L*ook for this mouse-sized bird as it spirals its way *up* tree trunks, looking for ants, beetles, insect eggs, moths, spiders, bees and anything else hiding there in the nooks, crannies and crevices. An extra-long and extra-stout tail—really too big for a bird of such small size—braces and balances the creeper as it climbs. When a creeper reaches the top of his journey, he flies down to the base of the next tree and starts over.

This is an interesting feeding strategy, perfectly complementing the nuthatches that creepers are often seen with in winter mixed flocks. The nuthatches work their way down, the creepers work their way up; both types of birds find food, and all the angles are covered.

Creepers are common, but seldom seen. One reason for this—they are forest dwellers, although they will come to your garden, usually in winter (see tips). Another reason: Sometimes the only way to see a creeper is to catch a glimpse of its silhouette as it comes around the side of a tree on its spiral ascent. Then you may be able to follow the bird's progress if you watch closely. But don't take your eyes away—the mottled, brown-and-gray back camouflages the bird perfectly against tree bark.

Brown creepers don't seem extraordinary, but they are interesting to watch if you can find one—and it is often a challenge just to see one. Go out to the winter woods and look extra-closely when you find a mixed flock of chickadees, nuthatches and downy woodpeckers working the cover.

One way brown creepers do stand out though, is in the elaborate courtship display created by the male. He will fly a quick spiral around a tree trunk, in hopes of attracting a female. If he is successful, they will repeat the spiral, ascending flight many times before pairing off for breeding.

TIP: Smear peanut butter on a tree to attract brown creepers and give them something extra-special to find, and come back to again, in your garden. Smear the peanut butter on and in from the bottom up, the same way the creeper will approach it. Alternatively, use a peanut butter feeder as shown.

IDENTIFICATION

A small (5 to 5½ inches), drab bird with a distinctive, narrow bill that curves downward and is perfect for probing crevices and furrows in bark. The back is mottled brown and gray (perfect camouflage against bark), while the belly is creamy or white. The call is a very high-pitched, lisping *tsee*, often given as the bird flies down from one tree to the base of the next. The song is a rather weak series of whistling warbles, most often heard in spring.

NESTING

Good luck finding a brown creeper nest. It is almost always strategically hidden behind a flap of loose bark—a cup of twigs, tiny sticks, bark shreds and moss. The parents often line it with feathers as a soft bed for the 5 or 6 white, brown-speckled eggs the female lays there. She handles all incubation duties for the 14–15 days it takes to hatch the eggs, but the male helps feed the hatched young until they fledge after 13–14 days and then start their own life cycle of working the trees.

TIP: Since creepers feed on animal matter, suet is also good for attracting the birds, especially in winter when they have to range a little farther and wider to find a meal.

TIP: Brown creepers like to hang out with the mixed flocks of birds that patrol the winter woods. If you see chickadees, nuthatches and woodpeckers on the prowl, look closely and listen for creepers too.

House Wren

Troglodytes aedon

An energetic but quirky little resident of summer gardens across the land.

Sometimes I wonder why I put up wren nesting boxes at all, at dawn on a summer morning with the windows open and a cool breeze drifting through. And then they start. Wrens! Singing—loudly—their bubbly-gurgly-trilling song and waking me up. But it's a very happy song, full of energy and life and a little mischief too. So I get up as well, to start my own busy day.

Aside from the early-morning singing, which has its pluses and minuses, one of the benefits of having wrens around is that they love to eat bugs—insects of all kinds, spiders, slugs, and caterpillars of all descriptions; many of these are pests you don't want around anyway.

Another benefit is being able to watch their quirky nesting behavior. The male starts by locating several holes or cavities (they love nest boxes—see attracting tips) in which to build nests. He will stuff the hole as full of sticks as possible; if the hole is in a nest box that was used before, he will excavate it and then fill it back up again—often with the same sticks!

Sometimes it seems as if there would hardly be room for a mother wren, not to mention eggs and then youngsters, in the place. But these nests become a dowry of sorts for him to show off to a prospective mate. If she chooses one, they're set. She will settle in quickly, adding her own finishing touches—a lining of soft plant material and feathers. The male is sort of a philanderer—he'll attract a second mate if he can, for another nest. Why let it go to waste?

TIP: Put up nest boxes to attract nesting wrens. They're not picky about the style, and they seem to take to hanging nest boxes very well. But the size of the entrance hole is important—it should be tiny, at 1⅛-inch diameter, for the male to accept it. Place nest boxes as close to your house as you want.

House wrens are rather aggressive birds, and that may be one drawback to having them around. They will chase off other birds—both wrens and other species, even birds that are bigger—to protect their territory. And, if other birds are nesting near where a wren wants to set up housekeeping, he will pierce the other bird's eggs; the goal is to reduce what will ultimately be competition for the insect larder of the surrounding yard and garden.

TIP: To feed wrens, try placing out some mealworms or other grubs, available at fishing bait stores or pet stores. Wrens are full-time meat eaters, and this is a good way to help them feed a growing family.

IDENTIFICATION

The house wren is tiny—only 4½ to 5 inches long—and rather nondescript. Both male and female are dusky-brownish above, slightly paler below. Look for the somewhat long, very sharp-looking beak and, especially, the tail that is cocked straight up, sometimes even flexing up and over the back. Listen for the babbling, musical song mentioned, high-pitched at first and then dropping lower and away.

NESTING

The male looks for almost any hole or cavity in which to cram his nest of sticks. Although trees are the natural place for these nesting activities, the aptly-named house wren has adapted exceedingly well to living around man, and will readily take to a nest box. Some of the oddball places wrens have nested include: mailboxes, overturned flowerpots, a sock on a clothesline, and gutter spouts that are somehow plugged upstream. The female lays and incubates 6 to 8 white, brown-speckled eggs. The young hatch in 14 days and fledge 15 days after that. She will try to raise 2 or 3 broods in a summer. In defense of the philandering male, he will take over the duties of feeding and raising the young if the female goes off to find her own new love.

TIP: Identify a house wren from other wrens by the light ring around his eye, and no striping on the face.

▶ Inset: This wren is taking an insect meal to her young in a tree cavity.

Gallery of Wrens

Though the house wren is most common and widespread, other wren species have evolved to fill different habitat niches. There are wrens for some of the steepest, rockiest, sharpest, warmest, driest and wettest places you can imagine.

Canyon Wren

Catherpes mexicanus

This wren of the badlands and canyons of the West and Southwest loves sheer cliffs and drop-offs for habitat, and nests in crevices and cracks in the rock. The canyon wren is darker than a house wren, with a white throat and breast.

Rock Wren

Salpinctes obsoletus

Rock wrens inhabit about the same range as canyon wrens, but seem to prefer rocky hillsides and slopes. They still nest in rocky crags and breaks (below). The rock wren is pale brown, with a finely streaked breast.

▲ Rock wren nest.

Carolina Wren

Thryothorus ludovicianus

A wren of the East, chiefly from the Ohio River valley down through the Carolinas and the Deep South. A Carolina wren is just slightly larger than a house wren, has a more reddish-brown coloration and sports a prominent white line above and behind the eye.

Cactus Wren

Campylorhynchus brunneicapillus

The cactus wren sings beautifully from his perch on a cactus spine. Cactus wrens also nest there in the cactus, in holes that are efficiently protected by spiny warnings. The cactus wren is quite large, at about 8 inches, and has spotted underparts, a speckled brown-and-white back and a rusty-brown cap.

Marsh Wren

Cistothorus palustris

If you see a wren in a marsh, cattails, bulrushes or other wet area, chances are it's a marsh wren. He is about the size of a house wren, a little darker, but the prominent features are the white striping on the back and the prominent white eyebrow. There is also a short-billed version of this bird, *Cistothorus platensis*, also called the sedge wren.

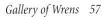

Ruby-Crowned Kinglet

Regulus calendula

A *tiny, red-capped traveler* that loves to eat insects.

Kinglets are about the size of the largest hummingbird, and that means they are one of the smallest of our North American songbirds.

Although the ruby-crowned kinglet and his cousin the golden-crowned kinglet (see below) are infrequent visitors to feeders, they are nevertheless common visitors to the garden at various times of year. They are highly attuned to forest habitat.

TIP: The ruby-crowned kinglet wears no face pattern. This is a good way to tell the bird apart from a golden-crowned kinglet.

That's where you'll see kinglets most frequently—in the trees, hunting for insects and spiders they pick from leaves and twigs. One interesting hunting strategy: ruby-crowned kinglets often hover in mid-air, plucking their prey off foliage. They will even grab insects in flight, while both insect and bird are flying. This particular behavior often causes the kinglet to be confused with migrating warblers, but there are ways to tell them apart (see identification notes).

If you live in the South, you're likely to be visited by ruby-crowned kinglets in the winter, when you can find them in deciduous forests, wooded bottomlands and treed gardens and backyards in both country and city. After winter, kinglets move north to nest in the coniferous forests of Canada, right on up to Alaska and the Arctic. Quite a trip for so tiny a bird! In the West, kinglets will stay as residents year-round, in areas where mountain and foothill coniferous forests offer the nesting habitat they prefer.

IDENTIFICATION

An overall olive-gray bird with dark wings and prominent white wing bars. Look for the broken white eye ring, as well as the stubby tail. The best way to discern the bird from a female warbler is (if you can spy it) the tiny patch of red on the head. This red crown is small, and beautiful indeed, but unfortunately hard to see because the owner, always the male, only erects it when he is feeling excited (as in courtship) or aggressive. A kinglet nervously flicks its wings too, another trait that sets it apart from the warblers. Listen for the call, a rough *jit-jit*, and the surprisingly loud song for such a little bird; high-pitched to low-pitched, it goes *chee-chee-chee chew-chew-chew chidee chidee chidee.*

NESTING

Six to 9 creamy-white eggs, blotched with brown or gray, reside in a moss- and feather-lined cup of moss and rootlets, built in the bough of a conifer. The baby kinglets hatch in 12 days, and fledge 12 days after that. They are raised on a high-protein diet of insects before venturing out on their own, tiny packages alone in the world.

Golden-Crowned Kinglet

Regulus satrapa

The golden-crowned kinglet wears a conspicuous face pattern, with a white eyebrow and a black stripe through the eye. The female's cap is golden yellow, the male's orange; a black line separates the colored cap from the white eyebrow mentioned. Golden-crowned and ruby-crowned kinglets approach life in much the same way—they nest in the North (usually in conifers), eat insects and spend winter where it's a little milder. However, the golden-crowned kinglet is better known for staying farther north in the winter—often as far as the northern tier of states and southern Canada—where he will forage with the cold-weather mixed flocks of chickadees, nuthatches, woodpeckers and company.

Red-Eyed Vireo

Vireo olivaceus

Champion singer of the summer woodlands.

For as widespread as the red-eyed vireo is, you'll talk to a lot of people who have never seen one. That may be a little surprising, because this vireo—by far our most common one—inhabits deciduous forests almost everywhere in the U.S., save for the central and southern Rockies. In the plains and prairies, you'll find red-eyed vireos in the riparian (riverbank) forests.

You'll have to go out in the forest, take a little walk, and listen, to start on your road to seeing a red-eyed vireo. The song is robin-like but shorter, very musical, and repeated almost endlessly. One study revealed an individual singing almost 20,000 of these musical lilts in one day.

The vireo will even sing as it decapitates and eats an insect it has caught. Even on the hottest of days, you'll hear this performer singing his song. Once you hear it, watch in the trees. Soon you'll see him, mostly olive (hence the species name *olivaceus*) with distinctive face markings as described in the identification notes, and that striking red eye.

TIP: Facial markings (including an eyebrow bordered by black) and a red eye positively identify this vireo.

Red-eyed vireos are relatively abundant, but they are not without threats to their well-being. One challenge is deforestation that seems to be on the upswing again as urban and suburban areas sprawl. Another threat is the brown-headed cowbird, an insidious pest that lays its eggs in other birds' nests, letting the little vireo parents unknowingly put all their energy toward feeding the monster that hatches; red-eyed vireos seem to be preferred targets in this respect. Finally, as a neotropical migrant, red-eyed vireos return to less and less rain forest each year when they migrate to Central and South America, often all the way to the Amazon, to winter.

IDENTIFICATION

An olive-green bird, about 6 inches long, with a narrow, white eyebrow that is bordered by black above and below. The lower black stripe is at eye level. The crown is gray. The eye is deep red, but you have to be fairly close to see it. There are no wing bars. Young birds do not have the red eye, but retain a brown iris until they reach about their first birthday. See song notes at left.

NESTING

Like all vireos, the red-eyed vireo weaves a deep cup of bark strips, grasses and lichens, suspending it from a couple of forked twigs at the end of a branch (see inset photo next page). In this secluded hideaway, the female incubates 3–5 white eggs that are peppered with dark brown and black. The young hatch in 12–14 days, and then fledge only 10–12 days after that. The parents will then try to raise a second brood, a frequent strategy of neotropical migrants who have to make as many offspring as possible when the making is good.

▶ Inset: Red-eyed vireo female at nest.

White-Eyed Vireo

Vireo griseus

The white-eyed vireo, though fairly common, limits its spring and summer travels to east of the Mississippi. There it sticks to thickets, brambles, undergrowth and brush more than its red-eyed cousin of the mature woods. How to tell the two apart? The eye of course, is white on this bird (once it reaches adulthood). But you often can't see the eye well enough to discern color anyway, especially in the shadows of thickets and woods, so look for yellow-green flanks, white wing bars and yellow "spectacles" around the eyes. Nesting strategies include the typical vireo cup, woven and suspended from a couple of twigs. Fledging takes especially long for white-eyed vireo young, 20–25 days.

Thrushes & Other Large Songbirds

Here is a wide variety of garden songbirds—an array full of stunning color, simple elegance, and fascinating habits and life strategies. True, many bird families are represented here, the only common thread being that these are larger citizens of the yard, garden, forest and field. Some of these birds may only rarely visit your garden. But if you decide to go elsewhere bird watching—either another type of habitat near home or to a place far from home—you'll be glad you learned the basics of identifying and understanding that bird right here.

Here's to the astounding variety of beauty and survival strategies that the bird world represents.

American Robin

Turdus migratorius

A familiar, popular—and interesting—visitor to yards and gardens.

*I*f any bird needs little introduction, it's the American robin. With its beautiful, lilting song (a sure harbinger of spring), handsome good looks and willingness to live and raise young in yards and gardens, the robin holds a special place in many bird lovers' hearts. But that familiarity can also mean that we often look past all the interesting adaptations and behaviors that make a robin a robin—and so successful at life, even in today's world.

Before our country was settled, the robin was, for the most part, a resident of woodlands and woodland edges. As settlement advanced westward, the robin adapted well and even moved out onto the prairie as the sod was broken. We often forget that the robin originated as a bird of the wilderness, and you can still find wild populations today, deep in the woods and fields. These birds have always seemed bigger, more richly colored and wilder to me—and definitely more wary and elusive—than their city and suburb counterparts.

The robin is a fruit eater—another fact bird lovers are sometimes unaware of, thinking of this lawn roamer as strictly an earthworm eater. But robins love berries of all kinds—crabapples, plums, mulberries, sumac, cherry, wild grapes, virtually anything that's in season or (if it's winter) still on the tree or stalk. At nesting time, robins become skilled insect hunters, to provide their babies the high-protein diet they need to develop quickly.

As for worms—almost everyone is familiar with the picture of a robin shuffling along and pausing ear to the ground listening for earthworms. But the bird is not listening—with eyes on the side of his head, this is the only way he can see the worms in their holes.

Many robins, especially the country kind, are willing winter residents across much of the birds' range—especially if the winter is a relatively mild one, and good amounts of the previous summer's fruit and berry crops remain on trees. But no matter what season you observe him, take some time to really appreciate the robin and all his adaptations to life in wilderness as well as cities and towns.

TIP: Robins love fruit—crabapples, plums, cherries, chokecherries—and planting this type of small tree or shrub will bring many robins to your yard.

TIP: Minimize chemical usage on your lawn, opting instead for more organic means of fertilizing and pest control, to help robins and other lawn-feeding birds. Keeping your lawn mowed to an appropriate height—but not scalping it—will help robins hunt.

TIP: Although not easily attracted to feeders, one way you can help robins is to erect a nesting platform on a tree or building (see inset photo on next page). Birdbaths also bring regular visits from robins.

IDENTIFICATION

The familiar robin measures from 9 to 11 inches, from tip to tail. This is the size by which almost all other songbirds are judged; for instance, you'll hear another bird described as "smaller than a robin" or "robin-sized" or "noticeably larger than a robin" or something similar. Look for the orange-ish, brick-red breast below; gray back and wings; and darker head. The beak is yellow. Males are hard to tell from females, but if you have a pair next to each other, a darker head and richer, deeper breast coloring will identify the male. The young have spotted breasts. Listen for the beautiful *cheerily-cheerily-cheerily* song bright and early in the morning and again in the evening, as well as the *chut-chut-chut* call of feeding birds.

NESTING

Robins love to nest near people it seems, and they are one of the few birds with this habit that we seem to tolerate. The female builds the nest herself, anywhere from 5 to 25 feet above the ground and usually in the fork of a tree or shrub, on the ledge of a building or garage, on a windowsill … most anywhere that offers a solid platform. Robins seem to like protection from the elements, and don't hesitate to commandeer nesting spots under eaves, overhangs or decks. The female builds the nest of twigs and grass, lining it with mud and then forming a cozy cup with her body, while the mud is still wet. There she incubates 4 or 5 pale blue-green eggs that hatch in 12–14 days and fledge 14–16 days after that. The male contributes by feeding her, and then helping supply the nestlings with insects, caterpillars, spiders and other protein. He also staunchly defends the couples' small territory, sometimes fighting with his reflection in a window. A pair will often try for a second brood.

Eastern Bluebird

Sialia sialis

Stunning resident of meadows, parks and gardens, in a coat of blue and rusty orange.

To see a male bluebird is to see a piece of the sky flitting about the trees and grassland.

A dyed-in-the-wool insect eater, you will usually see a bluebird—either a bright male or the more subdued but still pretty female—hunting for insects from a perch low on a fence post or wire, or tree branch. This bird loves open areas, grasslands and meadows with trees scattered about, and farmland, orchards, parks, cemeteries, roadsides—even backyards make decent habitat—as long as there are insects and places to perch around, and places to nest.

All that seems simple, but the bluebird is experiencing challenging times on both these fronts. As for food, insects are essential, and pesticides not only remove insects from being available at all, but the chemicals also poison the remaining insects, and that residue ends up harming adult and young bluebirds alike.

Fierce competition for nest sites is probably an even bigger reason for the bluebird's decline—namely aggressive, non-native starlings and house sparrows that, like the bluebird, are cavity nesters and either take up spots bluebirds could have occupied or just kick the bluebirds out and take over. To add to the problem: As land is cleared and otherwise cleaned up, old dead trees and snags are removed—further reducing the availability of appropriate nesting spots to all the species who love them, bluebirds included.

The biggest things you can do: erect and monitor nest boxes, eliminate harsh chemicals and pesticides from your gardening, and let some areas of your garden go a little wild. Plant fruiting trees and shrubs—and berry bushes too—for bluebirds like fruit as well as insects, especially early in the season when they return to the nesting grounds but insects haven't yet hatched and some of last year's fruit remains.

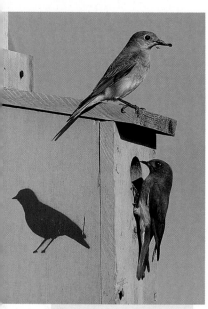

TIP: Put up bluebird houses. A hole of 1½ inches in diameter is important for keeping unwanted starlings out. Place the house 4 to 6 feet above the ground, with the opening facing north, east or northeast to prevent heat build-up in the home. Check your houses once a week, and clean out the nests of sparrows or other unwanted invaders; they can find another spot.

IDENTIFICATION

There's no mistaking a male bluebird—he is bright blue above, seemingly bluer than the sky—with a lovely chestnut-red breast and a white belly. The female is attractive too with her duller plumage on top—a light gray with accents of pale blue usually—along with a rusty-red wash of feathers on a paler breast, above the white belly. Like other thrushes, the young have spotted bellies. Adult eastern bluebirds measure about 7 inches, so are a little smaller than robins. The bluebird brings a beautiful song to accompany its stunning good looks—a musical *churlee-churlee-churlee*.

NESTING

The eastern bluebird nests in cavities, so if you have any old and rotting trees around, by all means leave them up! Erecting nest boxes is a good idea whether you have old trees or not. No matter what the cavity, a male will take a female on a tour of potential sites, and she will build the nest after selecting one site. The male will vigorously defend this site against other bluebirds and, as best he can, more aggressive invaders. The female lays 4–6 pale blue eggs and incubates them for 13–15 days. The male guards the nest when she is away, and joins in to help feed the voracious young. The pair hunts hard, bringing soft insects to the nest as often as every 5 minutes…hundreds of trips a day. The young fledge in 15–20 days, and there are few sights as sweet as a fluffy little bluebird making his or her first twittering flight to a fence post or wire.

TIP: Bluebirds eat insects, so are helpful in the garden. You can help bluebirds by minimizing or eliminating pesticide usage.

▶ Inset: Female eastern bluebird.

TIP: Set out some grubs or mealworms in a rimmed tray of most any type—even a garbage can lid works well—to give hunting bluebird parents an easy catch during nesting season. You'd be surprised at how readily the parents will take this offering, if they're in the area.

Mountain Bluebird

Sialia currucoides

The bluebird of mountains and the high plains, as blue as the western sky.

It is somehow fitting that the mountain bluebird male is entirely blue—as blue as the endless skies above the mountain and high-foothill strongholds he calls home. That home is usually a grassy meadow with scattered trees and shrubs. Look for an unbelievably turquoise-blue bird, about 7 inches long, with a slightly paler, gray-blue chest. The female is more subtly beautiful, with her gray, blue-brushed plumage.

Mountain bluebirds eat insects for the most part, like their eastern cousins, and have a unique hovering-style of hunting, riding air currents low to the ground before dropping down on insect prey. In autumn you can often see loose flocks of these insect hunters, along fencelines and roadsides in the West, flying gracefully and perching on fence posts and barbed wire as the birds migrate down from their alpine summer haunts, into the valleys and onto the plains. Fruits are a favored food when the insect crop freezes up.

TIP: Both mountain and western bluebirds nest in cavities, and will readily use the same types of nest boxes as their eastern cousins.

Western Bluebird

Sialia mexicana

A bluebird for the West Coast, bringing a rusty-red belly back into the mix.

Down the west slope of the Rockies and on to the coast, from British Columbia to Mexico, is western bluebird country. This bluebird loves the same kind of habitat as its mountain and eastern cousins—meadows with trees, bushes, scattered shrubs, and fences that provide plenty of perching spots for insect hunting.

It's easy to distinguish a male western bluebird from a male mountain bluebird (previous page). A western bluebird will have a rusty-red chest, along with that same rusty red on the back, and blue on the throat. A female western bluebird will have tints of orange in her plumage, compared to a mountain female. Western and eastern bluebird ranges do not overlap, so if you're in the Far West and see a bluebird with reddish or orange on it, it's a western.

Brown Thrasher

Toxostoma rufum

Secretive, handsome hunter of brush and thickets.

*I*f you're ever walking in the woods and spy a bright, rufous-colored bird hop-hop-hopping along, tossing leaves in the air as it goes, you're probably watching a brown thrasher out on a hunt for insects. In fact, he's named for just that habit—thrashing about in the leaves in quest for food.

You won't often see thrashers in the open, yet you won't find them in the deepest, primeval forest either. These are true creatures of the woodland edge, sticking closely to the denser side of openings and glades between fields and woods, meadows and woods, shelterbelts and fields, and yards and brush; urban thickets will attract thrashers too.

Thrashers consume about 75% insect food in spring and summer (spiders, crickets, beetles, ants, caterpillars, cutworms, moths and much more), the balance being made up by berries (blackberries, blueberries, raspberries, cherries and other fruit from dense shrubs), fallen fruit such as plums, and some grain and seeds. By fall and winter, when insects have hidden themselves away, the ratio flops to 75% plant food—

chiefly low-hanging and fallen fruit—for the thrasher prefers feeding on the ground.

It's always a pleasant surprise to see a thrasher hopping through a summertime thicket, and get a glimpse of that rusty-brown coat as he thrashes his way to another meal.

TIP: Brown thrashers stick to dense cover, flinging leaves out of the way in a perpetual hunt for insects to eat. Look for yellow around the eye.

TIP: Brown thrashers are often confused with wood thrushes. Here is how to tell the two apart: the thrasher has a yellow eye (versus black for a wood thrush), is slightly longer with a longer tail, has a streaked (not spotted) breast, and sports two white wing bars. The wood thrush has more of a rust-colored head.

TIP: The thicker the cover, the better for thrashers. Let a brushy corner get even brushier, let a hedge grow larger; you could even throw clippings and trimmings back on a hedge to make it shadier and denser and more attractive to thrashers.

IDENTIFICATION

A biologist might call it "rufous" but "rusty red-brown" would be the common description of this bird's primary color. A white belly with dark-brown streaks, along with a long, curved bill and a long tail, round out the distinctive package. Brown thrashers are a little longer than robins, at 10 to 12 inches in length, but appear more slender. Members of the mockingbird family, the brown thrasher will mimic other birds but usually sings its own song of couplets (short verses in pairs). When a thrasher is feeding, you'll hear a harsh *chack* call now and again.

NESTING

Thrashers will nest low in a bush (they seem to prefer thorny ones the most) or even right on the ground, building a rather unwieldy bowl of twigs, leaves and grasses lined with rootlets and moss. There, the female lays 3–6 pale blue, brown-spotted eggs that both parents take turns incubating. The young hatch in 12–14 days and fledge 9–13 days after that, heading out with the parents to learn the ins and outs of thrashing about woodland thickets.

Wood Thrush

Hylocichla mustelina

Quite possibly North America's most beautiful bird singer, and a woodland counterpart to the robin.

You'll find very little about the wood thrush in bird and birding publications, at least not to the extent you'll find information on the more "glamourous" species. In fact, many books don't even mention the wood thrush.

That's probably fitting, considering that this shy resident of dense, deciduous forests (usually near creeks, ponds or other moist areas, it seems) keeps such a low profile anyway. A wood thrush just likes to go about his business, hunting insects in spring and summer after returning from his Mexican and Central American wintering grounds. As summer wears on and fruit ripens, the wood thrush turns more to that type of forage—dogwood, elderberry, cherry, creeper, grapes, mulberries and so forth—before heading south again.

But that the wood thrush is not well known is also a little bit of a shame, because many consider him to be North America's finest singer. The song is a rich melody of clear, flute-like phrases, even more beautiful than a robin's carol. *Hee-o-lay, hee-o-lay hee*—lay is one way to describe the song, but doesn't really do it justice. A frequent scenario is that you'll hear the lovely singing but never catch a glimpse of the shy bird hiding way back in cover.

The wood thrush is the thrush world's answer for a citizen of the woodlands; he is closely related to the robin, but seems to prefer more and deeper cover. Yet the wood thrush seems well adapted to man's encroachment into the woodlands, and pairs are willing to nest near homes and in yards and gardens, just like robins.

TIP: In addition to letting woods be woods, here are two ways to attract thrushes. First—they love water, so place a bird bath close to cover. Second—appeal to their taste for fruit by placing out raisins, chopped prunes, even grapes, on a board or plate in a quiet location.

TIP: Wood thrushes stick to cover, preferring deep, moist woodlands for both general living and nesting.

IDENTIFICATION

The wood thrush is a very handsome bird, rich brown above with a rusty colored head, and a creamy white breast that is heavily spotted (not streaked) with brown to black. The wood thrush is similar in looks to the thrasher but there are ways to tell them apart (see page 70). At about 8 inches in length, the wood thrush, on average, is a little smaller than a robin but exhibits many of the same hunting behaviors in his woodland home. Like other thrushes, the song is lovely, but the bird also makes a series of distinctive *pip-pip-pip-pip* calls when working the woods for food.

NESTING

It's not too surprising that the wood thrush's nesting habits are similar to the robin's—a nest of twigs and grass, lined with rootlets and reinforced with a well-shaped cup of mud inside. The nest is usually 6–12 feet off the ground, in a convenient fork of a tree or shrub. There the female lays 3–4 blue-green eggs that she incubates for 14 days. The young fledge 12–13 days after that, learning to hunt insects on the forest floor and amongst the leaves and, at summer's end, turning to ripening fruit.

TIP: The wood thrush sings one of North America's most beautiful and melodious bird songs, usually from his hideaway back in the forest.

Gray Catbird

Dumetella carolinensis

A simple gray bird that often sounds like a cat, but creates a beautiful song as well.

*I*t would be hard to come up with a better name for this bird of thickets, brush and woodland edges.

First of all, the gray catbird is about as gray as a bird can get, save for his black cap and dark tail. Yet at the same time it's a very striking bird—on the rare occasions when you can actually spy one in cover or one makes a venture into the open—with its slender profile and big black eyes.

Then there's the "cat" part of the name: If you're ever in your yard or garden (or taking a walk or hike) and hear what sounds like a somewhat disturbed cat making harsh, raucous meows from a tangle of bushes, there's probably a catbird in there. Walk quietly, look closely, and if you're alone or don't think you'll embarrass yourself, meow back and the curious bird might flit over to take a look.

It's a treat to see a gray catbird, because they really do stick to thick cover, where they hunt on the ground for fallen fruits of all kinds, as well as insects. They seem to eat more fruit than insects, and it would be easier to list what fruits they don't eat versus all the ones they do.

Gray catbirds seem to do very well in urban and suburban areas, benefiting by disturbance to the land, which creates the thickets and brushy edges the birds love. Catbirds are friendly and can become somewhat tame once they get used to human presence.

The gray catbird may be somewhat nondescript in its looks, but it has a simple beauty all its own, and makes up for any lack of splashy plumage with its beautiful song, a tune of pretty notes and phrases running the scale. As a member of the mockingbird family, he likes to mimic other birds as well.

TIP: Lure catbirds out of the brush with some chopped-up fruit or raisins in a tray on the ground, or half an orange or apple impaled on a branch. Place the offering close to the edge of cover, as the catbird doesn't like to be more than a hop away from a tangle.

TIP: Catbirds love fruit: blackberries, blueberries, raspberries, cherries, plums, poison ivy, elderberries, gooseberries, mulberries, Virginia creeper, bayberries, holly … too many to continue!

Plant fruit-bearing shrubs such as those mentioned above, and let them grow into dense, easy-care thickets, to attract gray catbirds. You'll be providing cover, and food in the form of fruit as well as the insects that reside there.

IDENTIFICATION

Look hard into thickets and tangles for a slender and dusky-gray bird, a little smaller than a robin at 8 to 9 inches in length. The cap is black. The tail seems long for the bird, dominating a good portion of its total length. If you see a catbird in flight, you might also spy the rusty coverts under its tail. The top of the tail is dark. The easiest way to locate a gray catbird is to listen for its cat-like meowing as it hunts through a tangle of shrubs and vines for the fruits and insects there. The song is beautiful as well, as described at left.

NESTING

Male and female partners work together to build a nest, the male bringing the supplies (twigs, leaves, plant stems and bark) to the female. She masses it all together low to the ground, always in thick cover or even a tangle of vines within the cover, and then lays 4–5 shiny, blue-green eggs. She incubates them for 12–15 days, and then feeds the hatchlings with her partner for another 10–15 days before the youngsters fledge. They then follow the parents out to start learning about life in the thickets, trying to be secretive but meowing a lot, and hunting for fruits and insects.

Bobolink

Dolichonyx oryzivorus

This blackbird sings a bob-o-link song, and summers in our northern meadows and grasslands.

While the bobolink spends his summers in grasslands, fields, meadows and other open areas across the northern third of the U.S., he is a neotropical migrant. That means, during the spring and fall migrations, you might see him anywhere in the country.

Those trips got the bobolink in trouble in the late 1800s and early 1900s, when vast flocks of the birds would stop off at rice fields in the South during their autumn journey to the Southern Hemisphere. The "rice birds" were shot indiscriminately, and not many made the entire trip to southern South America. Of course, even fewer made it back the next spring due to other, more natural mortality.

Fortunately, the birds are now protected, and doing better where there are open grasslands and chances to nest undisturbed from mowing, hay-cutting and the like. It is those types of areas where you might see a breeding male in his upside-down tuxedo, or the more secretive, buffy-brown female. The male sets up a territory, performs an elaborate, fluttering display flight to attract females, and will court and breed with more than one partner. This last adaptation is important, for it allows multiple families to be raised in the best habitat, increasing the chances for a successful breeding season for the bobolinks.

Bobolinks eat mostly insects in the summer but, as alluded to, love grains and seeds in autumn and spring, when bug supplies are at lower ebb.

IDENTIFICATION

The breeding male is a rather handsome bird with his black chest, belly and sides; white back and rump; and creamy tan patch on the back of the head. A female (below) is much more camouflaged, looking very different with her buff brown feathers, and stripes on the crown and back. At 6 to 8 inches in length, bobolinks are a little larger than most sparrows. Look for the short, finch-like bill, and stiff, spike-like tail feathers. Listen for the gurgly, rolling song sounding like *bob-o-link bob-o-link bob-o-link*. When the birds are traveling, a good way to locate them is to listen for the nasal *pink* or *enk* call they will utter in flight.

NESTING

As described, bobolinks follow rather elaborate territorial and courtship practices for breeding. The nest is a haphazard but well-hidden bowl made of grass and stems, placed on the ground. There the soon-to-be mother will incubate 5–6 multicolored eggs (pale gray to brown and spotted with red-brown and purple) for 13–14 days, and the young will fledge 10–14 days after that.

▼ Female bobolink and young.

TIP: Bobolinks are birds of the open, summering in U.S. and Canadian grasslands, and wintering on the plains of southern South America.

You might attract a bobolink by spreading some grain—millet, oats, wheat, shelled sunflower—on the ground.

Dickcissel

Spiza americana

Friendly flocks in the heartland.

ere's a bird you don't hear a lot about. Yet its name, *americana*, says something about this bird's spring and summer home—the U.S. heartland, right on up into the Canadian prairie provinces. It is there—out in the grainfields, alfalfa fields, hayfields, meadows, and yards and gardens nearby—that the dickcissel returns each year to raise a family and spend the warm-weather months.

The dickcissel used to be fairly common to the east as well, but as woodlands have taken over where farming used to be common, the bird has retreated back to the central states and provinces.

A male dickcissel—handsome with his yellow breast with black "V," yellow eye stripe and chestnut wing patches, loves to perch on a fence post, lonely shrub or weed stalk, and sing his distinctive *dick-dick-cissel* song; the *dick* sounds are buzzy, the *cissel* sort of a hiss.

Dickcissels often gather in very large flocks for migration and, from a distance, these flocks look like huge waves. Some years it seems many birds return to the grasslands, meadows and fields they love, some years they are totally absent. Dickcissels are very gregarious; this can be attributed to groups sticking together in certain areas when conditions are good, stopping right there. The birds winter in Mexico and the northern portion of South America.

TIP: Dickcissels are birds of the open, and love to survey their surroundings from a good perch.

IDENTIFICATION

A dickcissel is approximately the size of a house sparrow, at about 6 inches in length. In fact, the females are often difficult to discern from a sparrow; look for a yellowish throat and breast and a longer bill to see if you can positively identify her as a dickcissel. A male dickcissel in breeding plumage is an interesting conglomeration of yellow chest, black bib, chestnut-colored shoulders and yellow stripe over each eye. Listen for the *dick-dick-cissel* song (details at left), or the buzzing *dzzzt* sound given in flight.

NESTING

The dickcissel needs open country for nesting—grainfields, grassy meadows, clover fields and hayfields—where a small nest of grass leaves and plant stems is built on or very near the ground. Dickcissel nesting success depends largely on whether or not their nesting area is mowed—a constant danger considering some of the habitat choices they are forced into. The male courts females from his perch atop a weed or fence post, singing his *dick-dick-cissel* song over and over. The female lays 4–6 light blue eggs that hatch in 12–15 days if the nest isn't destroyed by agricultural activities. The young dickcissels fledge about 2 weeks after that.

TIP: You may get some dickcissels to visit a feeder tray, especially at migration time. Sometimes they will visit with sparrows. Stock the tray with seeds like millet, cracked corn or sunflower.

▶ Inset: Female dickcissel.

Northern Mockingbird

Mimus polyglottos

Master of mimicry, lover of fruit.

Day or night, the mockingbird sings beautifully. Yes, even at night! The bird has a rich and lovely song of its own, a flowing series of musical phrases repeated three to six times. But apparently that isn't good enough for the mockingbird, who does not hesitate to imitate any other bird that shares its habitat.

This can be a good or bad thing, depending on your viewpoint. If you love to hear beautiful birdsong, it's good. If you're trying to identify singing birds, you might just be listening to an old mockingbird giving a concert. (One New England bird was documented to have 36 other species' calls or songs in his repertoire. Some males know over 150 songs in total—both theirs and mimicked ones.) Mockingbirds will imitate other sounds too—even cat meows, dog barks, toad croaks and piano notes they've heard through open windows.

Traditionally thought of as a Southern bird (it is the state bird of five Southern states), the mockingbird is steadily increasing its range northward, right on up through New England, the northern Midwest, even into Canada. The reason? The mockingbird loves residential and urban areas, and the fruit trees that go with them. Continued settlement of the land has created the lightly forested, broken habitat the bird prefers. It was originally named the northern mockingbird only because it resided farther north than any of its relatives.

Mockingbirds concentrate on fruit as the staple of their diet, switching over to primarily insects in spring or early summer only when the young have hatched and are fledging, and need a high-protein diet. Rose hips are a favorite food.

TIP: Mockingbirds love fruit, especially that of the multiflora rose, but most other kinds of fruits are eagerly gobbled as well.

IDENTIFICATION

Slender and graceful over its 9 to 11-inch length, the northern mockingbird is primarily gray—lighter below and darker above—with a bright yellow eye. The tail is long, and is white underneath. Likewise, the wings are white underneath; a mockingbird hunting for insects will flare those wings, presumably as a "flash" to startle and flush insect prey. The bird's Latin name, *mimus polyglottos*, means "mimics many songs," and that is the bird's chief fame, although they sing a wonderful song of their own (see left). Moonlit nights are favorite times for their serenades, and this night singing is a very unique trait among songbirds. Feeding mockingbirds give a loud *chack* call.

NESTING

Northern mockingbirds build a bowl of twigs, grass, weed stems and leaves, low in a shrub or tree. There, the female lays 4–5 blue-green eggs that she incubates for 12 days. Both she and the male defend the nest vigorously from intruders and predators. The young fledge 10–12 days after hatching, and the parents will often try to raise a second or third brood. The farther south you go, the more multiple-brood success mockingbirds will have.

TIP: To attract mockingbirds, place raisins or chopped apples on a feeder tray, platform, or your deck.

TIP: Mockingbirds hunt on the ground for insects, and concentrate on live prey during nesting season.

Cedar Waxwing

Bombycilla cedrorum

Sleek and elegant only begin to describe the beauty of this handsome, crested, black-masked songbird.

The cedar waxwing may well be our most beautiful songbird with its absolutely gorgeous, pastel plumage—brownish above and olive-yellow below—accented by yellow tail tips, bright waxy-red wing tips, black mask and pointed crest. In fact, the combination is so delicately lovely that in the late 1800s, cedar waxwings were almost exterminated because their cured, feathered skins were so valued as adornments on ladies' hatbands.

Fortunately tastes changed and the market gunning was stopped, and we still have this stunning bird with us today, along with all its wonderful antics. Most interesting is the bird's habit of lining up several-abreast on a tree limb or power line and then passing a piece of fruit on down the line until one eats it. Another habit: Although they love fruit the most, waxwings will hunt insects much as flycatchers do, snapping the bugs out of the air.

And cedar waxwings are wonderfully erratic in their travels, being here today and gone tomorrow as the group raids a ripe fruit crop and then moves on when the pickings thin out. If you see a cedar waxwing, enjoy him now because tomorrow he will probably be gone!

No one knows for sure why the wings have waxy-looking red tips, but they are prominent enough to give the waxwing its name.

To look out a window and see a group of cedar waxwings is almost like looking out at a battalion of little soldiers, all decked out in full dress and sporting the stripes of their rank. The birds love to travel in flocks of a dozen to even a hundred birds, and can be found in orchards, open woodlands, yards and gardens—wherever fruit is found. Waxwings have been known to become drunk on overripe, fermented fruit—tipsy enough that you can pick one up off the ground and cradle him until he sobers up. To gently hold such a bird must be like having a piece of feathered joy in your palms.

TIP: One of the best ways to attract cedar waxwings: Plant fruit-bearing trees and shrubs such as cedar (their favorite), juniper, crabapple, mountain ash, cotoneaster, chokecherry, bayberry, Russian olive, hawthorn and grapes.

TIP: Place small chunks of apple or figs, or raisins, at a feeder to attract fruit-loving cedar waxwings. The birds also enjoy birdbaths immensely, needing the fluids to help digest all that fruit and liking to splash around.

IDENTIFICATION

Cedar waxwings are unmistakable in their smooth, silky-looking plumage of brown above and olive-yellow below with yellow tail tips, crest, black mask and red, waxy-looking wing tips. Cedar waxwing adults average about 7 inches long—that's smaller than a robin—and waxwings are definitely sleeker and more slender. You will almost always find cedar waxwings in flocks. Listen for the call—a thin, lispy, trilling *tseeeee* as the birds roam for fruit or hover while hunting insects.

NESTING

Cedar waxwings like to nest in loose colonies, always close to a ripening fruit source that can help feed the growing family. The birds tend to nest later in the summer than most songbirds, when ripening fruits are more abundant than earlier in the season. The female incubates 3–5 blue-gray, black-spotted eggs she lays in a nest of twigs, grass, moss, leaves and hair. The nest is usually placed in a tree or shrub, and is fairly close to other nests. The eggs hatch in 12–16 days, and the chicks are fed a diet of insects and fruit. Adult waxwings can store much food—as many as a couple dozen berries, for instance—in their crops; they can then regurgitate the food to the hungry young back at the nest.

▶ Inset: A northern cousin, the Bohemian waxwing, is larger than the cedar waxwing and can be differentiated by the white wing patches, rusty-colored coverts under the tail, and belly that is more gray rather than olive-yellow. Flocks are big, sometimes numbering in the hundreds.

Blue Jay

Cyanocitta cristata

Rascal, robber and rogue, in a handsome topcoat of powder blue.

Few songbirds can inspire more of a love/hate relationship than the noisy, raucous and curious—but very intelligent—blue jay.

On the one hand, blue jays are large (compared to most feeder visitors) and do not hesitate to run off smaller, gentler visitors. This bully behavior can turn downright destructive too, for blue jays will raid other, smaller birds' nests and eat the eggs or young.

But don't judge the blue jay on those merits alone. Blue jays just do what blue jays evolved to do, and their redeeming qualities are many.

The blue jay is wise, resourceful and inquisitive, always seeming to be able to find a meal. In fact, the bird is steadily expanding its range westward toward the Rockies. The blue jay loves to stash tree seeds—especially acorns, many of which it forgets about—in the ground, so is an important planter of trees. Groups of blue jays take special delight in harassing predators such as owls and hawks, providing warning for other potential yard, garden and woodland birds.

TIP: A blue jay buries many seeds in its lifetime, many of which sprout into useful plants and even trees.

And blue jays are just downright beautiful, with their bright, powder-blue feathers, a black-and-white face and a large crest that stands erect when the bird is excited or being aggressive.

Blue jays are true omnivores, eating plant food (especially tree seeds but also many fruits in season) as well as animal matter (insects, bird eggs, and occasionally a small bird). Oak forests are preferred habitat, as are yards, gardens and parks in town.

TIP: Intelligent, aggressive blue jays will visit almost any feeder, but they seem to especially like black-oil sunflower seed. Spreading cracked corn on the ground will also attract jays.

IDENTIFICATION

You'll often hear a blue jay before you see it—listen for the harsh *jay-jay* cry; there is also a coarse but more musical *kwee-d-dle, kwee-d-dle*. The blue jay can sing too, and mimics other birds. Of course, there's no way to mimic the beauty of a blue jay— bright blue above and white below, with black-and-white bars on the wings, black markings around the face and a blue crest. The blue feathers are actually gray, but sunlight or natural light relecting off them gives them their spectacular powder blue color. Blue jays average about 12 inches long and have fairly substantial wingspans; couple that size with the bright coloration and noisy nature, and the birds are hard to miss.

NESTING

A pair of blue jays won't win any nesting derbies with their haphazard cup of sticks and twigs that is lined with leaves and grass. This nest is often placed in a conifer tree or other concealed tree fork or branch. The female lays 4 or 5 green, brown-spotted eggs there, and the parents make up for the poor housing by being especially territorial and protective of the nest area, even divebombing human intruders. Both parents share incubation duties for 17–18 days, and the young fledge about 20 days after that.

Gallery of Jays

When successful, Nature doesn't miss an opportunity to repeat a good idea. That's why we have these jays as well— to fill the open niches in brushland, boreal, mountain and desert habitats.

Scrub Jay

Aphelocoma coerulescens

The scrub jay is closely related to the blue jay, but occupies brushy, scrubby habitat in the Southwest. Oddly, there is a population in Florida, in scrub oak habitat that was probably once part of a broad, continuous, southern band of the brush. A scrub jay has no crest, the wings and tail are solid blue (no black or white markings) and the back is gray/brown. The scrub jay also wears a dusky-gray mask around the eyes. Scrub jays aren't quite as aggressive as blue jays, but will still take the occasional egg or young bird in addition to the acorns, nuts, seeds, fruits (see photo below) and insects they otherwise eat.

Gray Jay

Perisoreus canadensis

This is the jay of coniferous forests of the Far North and the Mountain West. The birds are gray above and white below, and have a white forehead and throat. There is a black nape on the neck, with a black stripe extending through the eye. If you've ever camped in the Northwoods or alpine West, you would know this bird as "camp robber" (see photo below) for the birds are very tame and will often come right up to you to take food. One interesting behavior: gray jays will use their saliva to bind together a mass off conifer seeds and store them for use when times are tough. Other common names include "Canada Jay" and "Whiskey Jack."

Steller's Jay

Cyanocitti stelleri

This jay is closely related to the blue jay (note the same genus name) and the two interbreed where their ranges overlap. The Steller's jay resides in the West's pine forests, where he eats seeds and insects, as well as acorns, other nuts and bird eggs in season. The Steller's jay sports a much deeper blue color than the blue jay, a sort of cobalt blue that blends into purple or almost black on the head and crest. Black bars adorn the wings and long tailfeathers. Steller's jays become tame around people, and will visit campsites for handouts, as well as yards for nuts, meat scraps and suet (see photo at right).

Eastern Meadowlark and Western Meadowlark

(Sturnella magna and *Sturnella neglecta)*

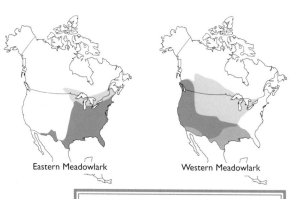

Eastern Meadowlark   Western Meadowlark

Bright and cheerful singers of meadow, field, prairie and open country.

Although not a regular feeder visitor, no bird book is complete without something about the meadowlark. These are birds of the open country—grasslands and prairies in the West, fields and meadows in the East.

With most species that have western and eastern versions, it seems to be the eastern version that is spreading west, but the opposite has occurred with meadowlarks: the western cousins have come east as woodlands were cleared and more land became suitable habitat.

Meadowlarks love to perch on fence posts. Fortunately, there is no shortage of these posts in either western ranch country or eastern farmland. From there, the meadowlark will sing its telltale song. That song is probably the best way to tell the two species apart, in fact.

The western meadowlark sings a complex song, a flute-like, bubbling series of notes that goes from high to low tones, a sort of *wee-chir-weedle-ee-ee-chee.* The eastern meadowlark's song, on the other hand, consists of three or four simple, mellow notes, a cheerful-sounding *see-you, see-here.* The calls are also different: the western's a low *chuck,* the eastern's a rattling, buzzy *dzzrt.*

From its fence post perch, or a perch atop a sturdy stalk of grass or prairie shrub, a meadowlark will hunt for insects, the mainstay of its diet. Meadowlarks will glean grain though, if given the opportunity.

TIP: Meadowlarks will frequently flush from the grass as you walk through a field or meadow, startling you. (Shown: Eastern meadowlark.)

TIP: Meadowlarks love open country, and fence posts are preferred perching spots. Barbed wire fences offer good perches too.

IDENTIFICATION

John James Audubon identified the western variation as a separate species in 1844, and named it *neglecta* because of the longstanding oversight. All meadowlarks look similar—streaked tan and brown above, yellow below, with a long pointed beak and a black "V" on the chest. You'll find them in open country—field, meadows, pastures and prairie. It's hard to tell an eastern from a western meadowlark by looks alone, but the western lark's yellow may be paler (a function of the more arid country it prefers), and that yellow may extend up into the cheeks. The best way to tell the two apart is by listening to the song (described at left).

NESTING

A male meadowlark will set up a territory that it will defend from other males, but he will allow several females to nest there if he can attract them. The meadowlarks will then build a cup of grass and weed stems at a low spot in the field or meadow, and even add a dome over the top. The female will enter from the side, and incubate 3–7 eggs for 13–14 days. Once the young hatch, fledging takes 11–12 days. Meadowlarks in farm country, as well as the irrigated lands of the West, have the unfortunate tendency to try to nest in hayfields and meadows, where mowing machines will destroy nests and eggs. The meadowlarks will try again if it's still early enough in the season.

▶ Western meadowlark.

TIP: Meadowlarks seem to be adapting to suburban areas better and better. They like fairly large expanses of open field or meadow, and they may come to scattered grain such as crushed corn, or wheat or oat kernels.

Northern Oriole

Icterus galbula

A striking orange-and-black bird, surprisingly easy to attract to your yard and garden.

The northern oriole presents an interesting dichotomy. In the East resides the race formerly known as the Baltimore oriole; in the West you will find the bird previously called the Bullock's oriole. These birds were once thought to be entirely different subspecies until biologists realized the birds freely interbred where their ranges met in the plains. The result: one species—the northern oriole.

No matter where you find them though, or what you call them, male orioles are stunning birds with their jet-black and bright-orange blend of plumage. As with most birds in the blackbird family (of which orioles are a part), the females are more drab-colored to camouflage them during nesting activities; in the oriole's case, she is olive brown above, a little lighter below with some traces of orange and yellow.

As you might expect from such a brightly colored visitor, orioles spend the winter months to the south, as close as Mexico or as far as Colombia. They must look right at home with all the other spectacular birds down in the rain forests, and that's probably what makes having orioles around so special. They are true symbols of summer weather, seeming to wait until spring is well under way, and warm weather assured, before making their appearance. Then they concentrate on eating insects, but they love fruit and nectar as well.

Orioles are fairly easy to attract to your yard or garden (see tips) and don't ask for a lot in the way of habitat, other than some mature trees. They love deciduous woodlands, and do well in suburbs, urban areas and neighborhoods, orchards, and city parks with mature trees. They loved American elm trees, but with the damage Dutch elm disease has wrought, orioles have turned to cottonwoods. It is interesting to note that cottonwood corridors, in the river valleys of the Great Plains, provided the treed habitat necessary to keep Bullock's and Baltimore orioles together as one species.

TIP: Slice an orange in half and set it outside, anchored on a nail or screw on a post, wooden deck ledge or anywhere, to attract orioles. Replace the fruit often to keep the food fresh and the orioles coming back. Commercial holders are also available for offering orange halves.

TIP: Orioles will eat grape jelly you place out in a tray. They also visit special oriole feeders (even hummingbird feeders) that offer sugar water.

TIP: Help orioles find nesting material: Place out pieces of yarn, fiber, string and threads that the birds can weave into their hanging-basket nest (see photo at right). Keep the pieces shorter than 8 inches to prevent them from tangling up and possibly strangling the bird.

IDENTIFICATION

Northern orioles measure 7 to 8½ inches long, about the size of a robin, but are more slender. The male's bright orange markings are unmistakable. A male oriole in the East has a black head, back wings and tail; the breast and rump are flame orange, as are shoulder patches. A male oriole in the West has orange cheeks and more white on the wings. Females in the East are drab olive-brown, with some traces of orange, and have two white wing bars. Western females are similar but have more gray on the back, and a whiter belly. In the plains, where the species interbreed, you can find wonderful variations on all this. Listen for an oriole's flute-like song—a whistling, very simple succession of four to eight *hoo-li* notes sung from the treetops. Both males and females sing.

NESTING

Orioles build nests that last. The female weaves a bag of plant fibers, string, yarn and bark strips, suspended from the tip of a branch high in a tree. There the eggs are relatively safe from the groping arms of raccoons, squirrels and other predators in this cozy, 6-inch-deep bag that is often 25 to 30 (but often as many as 60) feet off the ground. Males will set up and defend a territory of up to two acres around this nest, and will often return to the same area year after year to set up housekeeping. The female incubates 4–6 gray, blotched eggs for 14 days, and the young fledge 14 days after that.

Gallery of Orioles

Although lumping together Baltimore and Bullock's varieties into one species (the northern oriole) simplified the identification of orioles, it's still interesting to tell the two races apart. That's why we show representatives from both the Bullock's and Baltimore races here, as well as females from each. And there is also the separate orchard oriole to consider.

▲ Male.

▶ Female.

Bullock's Oriole

(Western race of the northern oriole species)

The Bullock's oriole evolved in the arid, open West so, as a tree lover, he naturally gravitates to the wooded areas along creeks and rivers, as well as towns with mature trees. The Bullock's loves to eat insects but relishes fruit (attract him with the tips given on page 90), and weaves a nest.

Baltimore Oriole

(Eastern race of the northern oriole species)

The original oriole, generally found in the first tier of states west of the Mississippi, eastward to the Atlantic. This is an oriole of the woodlands, although deep and unbroken forest isn't a necessity. These orioles seem to do fine in cities and suburbs.

◀ Female.

▶ Male.

Orchard Oriole

Icterus spurious

This oriole resides in the eastern half of the United States, with the core range seeming to be the true Southeast. But orchard orioles nest as far north as Minnesota and Wisconsin, and sometimes as far west as Colorado. Male orchard orioles sport an unmistakable chestnut color, nowhere near as neon-toned-orange as their northern oriole relatives. Females are olive-yellow, similar to northern orioles. Orchard orioles like to nest in colonies, and oak trees are a preferred habitat type.

Scarlet Tanager

Piranga olivacea

Bright scarlet resident of forests and treetops.

Your head will do a double take when you see a male scarlet tanager. The birds are that unbelievably, intensely red. "Scarlet" doesn't really do the color justice, but it's a start.

Although they're not common feeder visitors, scarlet tanagers show up in the yard and garden (and on summer bird walks) fairly regularly. Scarlet tanagers love woodlands, and your best chance of seeing one is if your yard and garden are well wooded, or you're out walking or berry picking in a block of forest.

You'll usually see tanagers well off the ground, all the way into the treetops, and sometimes it takes some glints of sun to be able to see the spectacular red color. The tanager spends much of its time there, high off the ground, foraging for insects (which it will hunt on the wing, fluttering out from its hunting perch) and fruits.

Scarlet tanager populations have suffered on a couple of fronts. One is the fragmentation of woodlands in the bird's summer range across the eastern United States. The birds need extensive unbroken tracts of woods. Valleys of the big rivers seem to be strongholds, where large tracts of forest can go on and on. Fortunately, scarlet tanagers will visit yards and gardens during migration time, in spring and fall, even if they're not going to stay. But they need big woods to make a season-long go of raising young. Another factor that has hit scarlet tanagers hard is clearing of the rain forests in Peru, Ecuador and Colombia, taking away precious wintering habitat where the birds winter.

If you see a male scarlet tanager in breeding plumage, you will long remember the color of those fiery, scarlet-red feathers. Drink it in while you have the opportunity, because the sighting is a very special event indeed.

TIP: Scarlet tanagers love deciduous woodlands—especially those with oaks—but will also do fine in parks, suburban areas, orchards and other areas that have a good smattering of mature trees, if extensive woodlands are nearby.

TIP: A scarlet tanager will visit a feeder where fruit—try chopped apples, figs or oranges—has been placed. Tanagers don't frequent feeders by any means, but the fruit will attract other species as well and if the offering stops one passing tanager for a few moments, the effort will be well worth it.

IDENTIFICATION

There is no mistaking the male in breeding—a gorgeous scarlet-red bird with black wings and tail. The female is olive-green above trending to yellow below, with darker, duskier-colored wings; the male reverts to this coloration after his autumn molt, before migration back south. The scarlet tanager measures about 7½ inches in length—smaller and more slender than a robin. Listen for the song, not unlike a robin's in its caroling tone, but a little hoarser. The male does most of the singing but the female will sing as well, before her egg-laying duties are complete. Tanagers also give a *kip-churr* call while feeding.

NESTING

A male scarlet tanager will employ a fairly sophisticated display show to attract a female to nest in the territory he has chosen. The birds locate the nest in a tree, usually a mature hardwood and almost always far out in the branches and at the end of a limb. The nest is a shallow cup of stems and twigs lined with grass. The female lays 3 or 4 pale blue or green eggs spotted with brown, and incubates them for 13–14 days. The young fledge 9–11 days after that and then the parents really kick into high gear, bringing high-protein insects back to the nest to get the youngsters raised and strong enough in time to make the long migration back to wintering grounds.

▶ **Inset:** Female scarlet tanager.

Western Tanager

Piranga ludoviciana

Color splash in the Rockies.

The East has the scarlet tanager, but the West is blessed with its own spectacular tanager, the western tanager. Bright yellow dominates the male's plumage, but he has a bright red head during the breeding season. The female is olive yellow, much like a female scarlet tanager (page 95), but you can identify a western female by her white wing bars. The male has white wing bars as well, and this is the only tanager species to bear this marking—a good identifier. At 6 to 7 inches in length, western tanagers are small, about sparrow sized.

It may be hard to spy a western tanager, because he loves the treetops, and hunts insects up there. Preferred habitat is conifer forest in the foothills and mountains of the West, all the way up to 10,000 feet in elevation. Fruits, buds and berries are also fair game in season; place out dried fruit or chunks of orange to see if you can get a western tanager to make a visit. The birds will also visit hummingbird feeders with perches, to sip nectar.

Summer Tanager

Piranga rubra

The South's own tanager.

The summer tanager rounds out the United States' tanager line-up. This is a bird of the South, though some birds nest as far north and west as Illinois, Wisconsin and Iowa. The male is rosy-red with a yellowish bill and no crest. The lack of a crest and any black facial markings quickly identifies him from a male cardinal, as does the light-colored bill (the cardinal's is red). A female is olive-colored above and a fairly bright yellow below; her wings are not dark as a female scarlet tanager's are.

Insects make up the bulk of the summer tanager's diet, and he hunts them on the wing. Summer tanagers prefer forest habitat, as well as yards and gardens with plenty of trees. These birds prefer higher ground over the lower, swampy forests of the South. Listen for the song from birds in the treetops they love to roam, a *tick-ticky-tuck* that is more musical than the scarlet tanager's notes.

Killdeer

Charadrius vociferus

Noisy but likeable, this plover lives inland.

The killdeer is actually a shorebird—a member of the plover family that lives out its high-energy, landlocked life in urban and suburban America, as well as open countryside. You can find killdeer across the United States, in warmer months. The name killdeer comes from the bird's telltale cry, a shrill and clear *kill-deer, kill-deer, kill-deer*, repeated many times. The bird's species name, *vociferus*, pays tribute to this loud, persistent voice.

Killdeer are creatures of the wide-open spaces—much like the ocean shore habitat of their plover cousins. But killdeer choose less exotic locations such as open parks and yards, playing fields, airports, plowed fields, golf courses and short-grass prairies. Trees are not needed. If killdeer are found near large water bodies it is coincidental; the birds evolved for life on land.

Their hunting technique is unique—a bird will run quickly for several feet then abruptly stop, and peck at the ground for any insect meal it can grab.

TIP: Killdeer nest right out in the open. The eggs are camouflaged well, almost invisible to the human eye.

Killdeer nest right out in the open, and have developed an interesting strategy for distracting predators. One of the adults will hobble off with a faked injury, spreading its tail and flapping its wings and acting for the world like it's about ready to keel over, all the while crying plaintively to keep the predator's attention. The predator will usually follow, and when the duped animal is far enough away from the eggs or nestling, the killdeer will fly off. If you're on a walk and get this treatment, step carefully and lightly to avoid crushing the almost invisible nest and eggs, and follow the actor directly away from the area.

TIP: Enjoy the show—and play along—when a killdeer feigns injury and attempts to lead you away from its nesting area.

IDENTIFICATION

The killdeer is a bird on the ground out in the open, 9 to 11 inches long (about the size of a robin with much longer legs, a throwback to the killdeer's shorebird ancestry). He is light brown above and white below with a rusty-colored rump. Two black bands across the breast identify the killdeer from other plovers. The bill is black. Look for the start-stop-start-stop hunting motion, and head bobbing. Listen for the loud and harsh-sounding *kill-deer kill-deer* cries.

NESTING

Killdeer nest right out in the open, in a small depression the female will scrape into the ground. There she lays 4 buff, blotched eggs. She and the male share incubation duties for about 24 days. The chicks are very well developed after this long incubation though, and they will fledge only 2 to 3 days after that; they need to be mobile quickly or be eaten by predators, since even with their camouflage they would be relatively easy to hunt, if immobile, in the habitat.

TIP: Killdeer love wide-open spaces. Mown lawns are a favorite habitat.

Belted Kingfisher

Ceryle alcyon

Little fisherman of lakes, rivers and creeks.

A kingfisher in action—hunting the minnows, tadpoles, frogs and aquatic insects that make up the bulk of its diet—is a spectacular sight. The bird might be sitting on a branch or wire over the water, or hovering. Then, with no preparation or indication of what's coming, the bird will drop and dive into the water, plunging in headlong and beak-first to grab its prey, which it will carry back to a perch to eat.

Back at the perch, the kingfisher will pound the prey silly, if needed, before eating it whole. You can often hear the crunching crayfish shells or fish bones. If they are training young ones, the parent will drop the dead catch back into the water for the youngster to "catch" on its own. Kingfishers will also eat lizards, salamanders, mice and even young birds; they are predators and will not pass up a free and good meal.

Kingfishers need water—lakes, rivers, creeks and even saltwater estuaries—to make a living. It also helps to have convenient perching places over water, where the birds can watch for prey. Some of these perches are natural—tree branches—while manmade additions also serve kingfishers well—like telephone or power wires. The perch must be fairly close to water though: not treetop height. A bird or pair will set up a territory and patrol a regular circuit of hunting perches throughout the area.

Kingfishers in the North migrate southward ahead of winter, before ice closes up their feeding grounds. Many birds will stay in the mid-South, only traveling far enough to find open water.

TIP: Kingfishers love to perch on a tree branch or wire over the water, watching for prey before dive-bombing in after it.

IDENTIFICATION

A striking bird, about 13 inches long (pigeon-sized), blue-gray on the back and white below. Both males and females have a blue-gray breast band; the female adds a chestnut-colored band, and has rusty-red flanks. Look for a bushy crest and a long, dagger-like bill that means business when it's time to fish for food. The call is a loud and raspy rattle. Look for birds perched over water—usually a shallow shoreline, or a riffle in a creek or stream, and watch for the dive and subsequent splash.

NESTING

The male and female will work together to dig a tunnel (up to 8 feet long) into a muddy or sandy-but-firm bank, and create a chamber at the end. There the female will lay 4 to 5 white eggs. She will incubate by day, he by night, for 12–14 days. After hatching, it takes 25–30 days for the young to fledge. The young kingfishers then have to learn how to hunt, from the parents (see above left). This process takes several days as well. All this work and time means a kingfisher pair can only raise one brood a season.

▶ Note the rusty, chestnut-colored band on this female belted kingfisher.

Loggerhead Shrike

Lanius ludovicianus

Meet the "butcher bird"—a songbird that's actually a bird of prey.

The loggerhead shrike looks like a songbird. But if you're a mouse, vole, shrew, small songbird, beetle or grasshopper, be afraid. For this black-masked bird is really an efficient predator, even without any talons.

A shrike will sit quietly in a bush or tree and wait for prey to come along, then pounce on the victim. The shrike uses its powerful bill to dispatch the hapless victim. Since shrikes do not have talons, they will frequently carry their catch up to a thorn or strand of barbed wire and impale the victim there so it stays stationary while the shrike rips it apart and eats it. Leftovers hang right there, and may be visited again if the carcass isn't entirely consumed. (This is the behavior that gives the loggerhead the nickname "butcher bird.")

Like other birds of prey, a shrike will occasionally regurgitate pellets made of fur, bone pieces, feathers and other indigestible matter. Although seeing a shrike is a treat, if there's one hanging around your bird feeding station you may lose a couple regular visitors. But that's all in the scheme of things; the hunting behavior from such a small bird is interesting to watch, and once your regular visitors get extra wary, the shrike will probably move on.

You can find loggerhead shrikes most anywhere in the continental U.S., with the birds wintering in the southern two tiers or so of states. Preferred habitat includes orchards, prairies, open areas with a few scattered trees, woodlands that are very open and grassy, and deserts. Shrikes like fence posts, fences and scattered trees as perching spots for their hunting activities.

TIP: Shrikes will impale their prey on a thorn or on a fence, then start ripping it apart from there. These small birds of prey don't have talons, as hawks and owls do.

Northern Shrike

Lanius excubitor

A very close relative to the loggerhead, the northern shrike resides in the Canadian tundra and Alaska during the spring, summer and early fall, but comes south to winter across southern Canada and the northernmost tier of American states. If rodent populations are at cyclical lows in the Far North, some northern shrikes will stay in the U.S. for the summer, presenting some interesting identification challenges (see identification notes).

IDENTIFICATION

The loggerhead shrike is a striking bird, 8 to 10 inches long, gray above and white below with a black facemask that stretches over the bill, and black wings. Watch for the low, fluttering flight and graceful swoops back up to a perch. The song is a series of harsh but musical notes and trills, a sort of *quee-dle-queedle* or *surp-ee surp-ee*. The northern shrike is difficult to differentiate, but a barred breast and a pale-colored lower mandible (versus black for the loggerhead) may provide the keys you need; also, the northern shrike's black facemask ends at the bill.

NESTING

Loggerhead shrikes like to place their nest in a thorny shrub or tree, building the mass from twigs and grass and lining it with feathers and plant down. There the female lays 4 or 5 white eggs that are splotched with gray or brown. Feeding the hungry nestlings is a full-time job for both parents, and they need good habitat in order to have enough prey to bring back to feed the family; insects are a staple food at this time, the bigger and juicier the better.

▶ Inset: Northern shrike.

American Crow

Corvus brachyrhyncos

Completely black and very smart, an adaptable survivor across North America.

*L*ike him or not, the crow is here to stay. As the plow and the town tamed North America's wilderness, the landscape got better and better for crows: plenty of crops to raid, more open areas in what was formerly woodland, more trees on what was formerly just prairie, more cars and then many roads to provide roadkill carrion. Today crows are common sights in urban areas, suburban parks and yards, farmland and woodland.

Crows eat what is at hand, and are true omnivores, consuming almost equal parts animal and vegetable matter over the course of a year. And as anyone who drives a car has noted, crows are often the first on the scene to start cleaning up what's left of a roadkill.

There is no doubt crows can be destructive to crops, especially corn. When a group of crows is feeding, one or two sentinels are posted to guard for danger as the rest of the flock forages. The birds are incredibly wary and catch on quickly to any attempts—such as hunting—to speed up their demise.

Crows have the destructive habit of raiding other, smaller birds' nests and eating the eggs or even the newly-hatched young. For this reason they are not always welcome in yards and gardens.

TIP: Crows eat a lot of carrion, but can also destroy crops.

One interesting little quirk: crows seem to like small, shiny objects and will steal them and carry them away to a secret hiding spot.

On the other hand, crows also provide at least one important service: they are willing predators of grasshoppers, cutworms, caterpillars and many other undesirable insects, in addition to their important scavenging activities.

Crows hate owls, and you can sometimes hear and then see a dozen or more crows harrying a poor owl from tree to tree during the daytime, trying to run it out of the turf they are currently calling home. Owls are efficient killers of roosting crows, and crows know it.

Once breeding season is over and winter is coming on and it's time to look for new food sources, crows will gather into groups of hundreds or even thousands of birds.

IDENTIFICATION

A jet-black bird from tip of beak to tip of tail. Crows measure from 17 to 21 inches long and are fairly bulky, so they make an imposing-looking package; this aids them in their aggressive behaviors. The bill is stout, and the tail is fan-shaped. (In contrast, the larger, common raven has a wedge-shaped tail. The common raven is essentially a larger version of the crow, and lives farther north and west.) A crow makes a *caw-caw* call with its raspy, loud voice; get a dozen or more crows calling together and you've heard the definition of the phrase *making a racket*.

NESTING

Crows build a bulky nest of sticks and twigs (usually in the fork of a tree), and then line it with feathers, leaves, grass, moss and anything else soft they can obtain. The female lays 4–6 greenish eggs that are spotted with dark brown, and incubates them for 16–18 days. Crows are large birds, so it takes a long time for a youngster to fledge—4–5 weeks. The young will usually stay with their parents through the winter, and sometimes for several years. Because nesting, fledging and training the young birds in crow ways takes so long, only one brood a year is attempted; the parents are very cautious and wary when nesting, and then very protective and attentive to the young.

Crows are very mischievous, and very loud.

Black-Billed Magpie

Pica pica

A long-tailed, black-and-white symbol of the West.

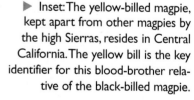

The great American West and magpies go hand-in-hand. A bird of rangelands, agricultural riverbottoms and wooded foothills (conifers are preferred), the magpie is part of the crow family and in fact occupies the particular niche crows would otherwise occupy.

This means that magpies steal grain, which sometimes causes them to be persecuted. But in a net sense it's probably better to have a few magpies around and let them have some morsels of grain now and again, for the birds are efficient predators of insects of all kinds, and mice. Magpies have also been known to sit on the backs of sheep and cattle, picking off ticks, lice and grubs to eat; one can only imagine that they did the same to bison when the giants still teemed on the Western plains and prairies.

But magpies will also rob the nests of other birds, especially ground-nesting gamebirds, and this can cause animosity toward the magpie as well.

So natural selection has made the magpie a very wary bird, and it's hard to approach one closely, even in a vehicle. The most common way to view them is to see their long-tailed silhouette gliding across a pasture or field, or the road in front of you. Many a pheasant hunter's heart has skipped a beat at seeing this, before realizing it's "just another old magpie."

The magpie just doesn't get a lot of respect. It's not that there's anything wrong with being a magpie. Although the bird is fairly common across the interior West, it really is a striking and handsome bird with bold black and white plumage, black bill, and purplish-green iridescent highlights in the sun.

TIP: A magpie will eat almost anything—from carrion to insects to mice to grains and even fruits when in season. Try spreading some bread on the ground to attract a magpie. Meat scraps, or leftovers from last weekend's roast, would also be relished by hungry magpies.

TIP: Magpies will come to suet.

IDENTIFICATION

A very long-tailed bird that totals from 17 to 21 inches in length. The head is black, as are the wings and tail, while the belly and a shoulder patch are bright white. The tail streams behind the bird in flight, and seems to have a greenish, iridescent hint. The bill is black. Magpies have a distinctive call, a rapid and nasal *yank-yank-yank* or *quig-quig-quig* that sounds very lonely in the empty spaces magpies call home. Look for magpies in open areas—cattle pastures, sagebrush, cropland and partially-forested foothills—across the West.

NESTING

A pair of magpies will mate for life, and they even prefer to use the same nest year after year for a go at raising another brood. So their bulky nest often continues to grow and grow, becoming a massive, domed pile of sticks and twigs that is lined with mud, plant material such as grass and rootlets, and hair. There the female lays 6–8 green-gray eggs that hatch in 22 days (the female does all incubation duties), with the surviving chicks fledging 22–27 days after that. A magpie will take another partner only if the other one dies or the two are separated permanently.

▶ Inset: The yellow-billed magpie, kept apart from other magpies by the high Sierras, resides in Central California. The yellow bill is the key identifier for this blood-brother relative of the black-billed magpie.

Warblers

Chances are that most of the warblers you see in your yard and garden will be migrant visitors— on their way to northerly nesting grounds in spring, or later traveling southwards ahead of winter. Almost all these birds are neotropical migrants, which means they winter in South America and then nest and spend the summer in North America. Think about the miles that bird has to fly—including a nonstop trip over the Gulf of Mexico—to get to where you can enjoy him or her.

Warblers are travelers extraordinaire, bringing flashes of the tropical warmth and color to the yard and garden. Enjoy them when you have them, for they will likely be gone tomorrow!

Yellow-Rumped Warbler

Dendroica coronata

A dapper, blue-gray warbler with swaths of cheerful yellow, formerly thought of as two species.

At one time, a book such as this would have listed two species here—the Audubon's warbler in the West and the myrtle warbler in the East—instead of just one yellow-rumped warbler. But as is so frequently the case with closely-related birds, ornithologists discovered that the two freely interbreed where their ranges overlap.

East or west, the yellow-rumped warbler is a dapper bird in his coat of blue-gray, with black-streaked breast and flanks, yellow wing patches, tiny yellow cap and yellow rump. The rump is the source of one term-of-endearment nickname: butterbutt.

If you're wondering whether the bird you're looking at would have been classified as a myrtle or Audubon's warbler, look at the throat: a myrtle has a white throat, an Audubon's yellow. John James Audubon named the western bird; the eastern version got its name from its love of myrtle berries, also known as bayberries.

Migration time is a treat for lovers of yellow-rumped warblers, for the birds will sometimes pass through *en masse* before moving on to nesting grounds in northern coniferous forests. In the West, the birds will nest in conifer forests at higher elevations.

The call is a single, sharp *chik* and the song is a buzzy, trilling warble.

Magnolia Warbler

Dendroica magnolia

A beautiful, black-and-yellow warbler of spruce, fir and pine woods.

At first glance, the pretty magnolia warbler might be confused with the yellow-rumped warbler. But upon a little studying, the differences become quite apparent: The color palette is the same, but the arrangement is very different.

For one thing, the magnolia warbler is bright yellow below, including the throat, with heavy black stripes on the underparts. Although it has a black face similar to the yellow-rump's, the magnolia warbler does not wear a crown patch of yellow. Finally, the magnolia warbler has a larger white wing patch, and a band of white across the middle of the tail.

The song is similar to the yellow-rump's, but is shorter, a sort of *weeta-weeta-weety*, with the last note rising. The call is one simple note, a *slip*.

The magnolia warbler actually has no special ties to magnolia trees, other than that when the bird was first identified in the early 1800s, migrating through Mississippi, specimens were collected near magnolia trees. Stands of young fir, spruce and other conifer trees seem to be the habitat type the bird really prefers, but you can see migrating magnolia warblers in most any type of wooded habitat. Migrations can be quite spectacular, with hundreds of birds streaming through for a few days and then they're gone, heading farther north to nesting grounds in the conifers.

Yellow Warbler

Dendroica petechia

Our most widespread warbler, in a yellow all its own.

A bird of thickets and second-growth woodlands, often near streams and swamps, this is probably our most widespread warbler. It is certainly one of our brightest and most beautiful.

Yellow warblers nest and spend their summers across the United States, except for the Far Southeast. If there are woodlands of any type around your garden, keep an eye out for yellow warblers.

These beautiful birds wear a yellow all their own—it's not the neon yellow of a goldfinch, but deeper and richer. This is the only warbler that is so overall yellow. The male also sports rust-colored streaks on his breast—the only part that isn't yellow save for the black eyes and some olive on the wings. A female is still yellow, but is a little paler and lacks the male's rusty streaks. The song is bright and happy and suitable for such a lovely summertime visitor, a sort of *sweet-sweet-sweet I'm-so-sweet.*

Yellow warbler nests are hit hard by cowbirds laying their parasite eggs, but fortunately a female yellow warbler will sometimes roll out the intruding egg, or build a new nest layer on top and start over.

Wilson's Warbler

Wilsonia pusilla

A tiny, black-capped warbler that hunts on-the-wing for insects.

The Wilson's warbler is a very small but very high-energy bird, usually found close to the ground where it darts on-the-wing after flying insects. In the East, the Wilson's warbler is a common springtime migrant through almost every habitat type, but especially woodlands and treed urban and suburban areas. In the West, the bird is quite common, especially along wooded streambottoms with plenty of brush, alders and willows.

A male Wilson's warbler is predominantly a dull yellow, but upon closer observation has olive wings. A black cap is prominent, and so is the beady black eye that has a patch of bright yellow above it. Females and young males have no black cap, but otherwise are colored similarly. Distinguishing both male and female Wilson's warblers from other warblers is fairly simple on paper but delightfully tough in the yard or woods: Wilson's warblers have no wing bars or streaks, or tail spots. Also, Wilson's warblers stay very close to the ground, usually within 12 feet. Listen for the chattering song—a fading series of *chips*.

The bird's name honors Alexander Wilson (1766-1813), a great American ornithologist.

Black-and-White Warbler

Mniotilta varia

This unique, striped warbler behaves more like a creeper or nuthatch.

Here's a warbler with the unique adaptation of creeping up (like a brown creeper) and down (like a nuthatch) tree trunks as it probes the bark's crevices, nooks and crannies for insects, larvae and eggs. While that behavior is distinctive, so are this warbler's striking markings: Both males and females are striped lengthwise with black and white. There is a white stripe down the middle of the bird's crown, as well as the back.

The female differs from the male only in that she is a bit paler. Look for the male's black throat during breeding season; but it turns white after the post-breeding molt. Listen for a thin, long and squeaky song, roughly translated as *we-see we-see we-see we-see*; some guidebooks describe it as sounding like a squeaky wheelbarrow.

Black-and-white warblers reside in deciduous forests, and nest across the entire eastern half of the U.S. on up into Canada. Some black-and-whites annually follow the wooded bottoms of the Missouri River out into the Dakotas. A few black-and-white warblers winter in Florida and along the Gulf Coast, but most head to northwestern South America; They are fairly conspicuous on their migration northward in spring, when you can see them in yards, gardens and parks that have mature trees. Because they don't require leafed-out trees for successful insect hunting in bark's nooks and crannies, black-and-white warblers return earlier than other warblers. After the migration thrust, head to the woodlands and listen for the song to track one down.

Chestnut-Sided Warbler

Dendroica pensylvanica

A warbler that has benefited from humans' changing land-use patterns.

lmost all warblers are migrants to some degree. This means habitat has to be right in two very distant places—summer nesting grounds in North America as well as wintering areas in Central and South America. The limiting factor has increasingly been declining wintering habitat as rain forest falls to the axe, fire and plow.

But here is a beautiful warbler that has prospered from better habitat and nesting areas here in the United States and Canada, as virgin forests were cut down and agricultural land use created brushy edge habitat. As much of that land continues to revert back to brush, overgrown pastures and scrubby second-growth woodland, chestnut-sided warblers have done even better. There were far fewer of these spectacular birds 200 years ago.

And a male chestnut-sided warbler is beautiful indeed: chestnut-colored sides, a bright yellow-green crown, and wings and back streaked with black and olive. There is a black stripe through the eye, as well as a black mustache. A female looks about the same except she is not quite so brightly plumaged. The song can be described as *pleased pleased pleased ta meetcha;* it is very musical, with the next-to-last note accented, the last note fading away into the thicket or brush the bird is singing from. Chestnut-sided warblers may nest in your area; at the least, watch for them during the spring migration.

Pine Warbler

Dendroica pinus

Warbler of the pines, perfectly named.

There is really no other suitable name for this unique warbler. Of course, the bird's habitat—exclusively pine forests, pine barrens or any other ecosystem dominated by pines—makes it unique. Pine warblers nest and spend most of their lives in the pines, hunting insects among the branches and needles or foraging close to the ground.

Another factor making the bird unique: Many pine warblers winter right here in the U.S., holding over in southern pine forests and plantations, as well as mixed woodlands with plenty of pines; you can see pine warblers hanging out with mixed flocks of nuthatches and chickadees at this time. But a few birds do go to the West Indies to winter.

This bird is also special among warblers in that, although it is pretty, it is not as gaudy as many of its cousins. A male pine warbler has a yellow throat and breast, with the breast only faintly streaked and fading to white the lower you go. The back and head are olive. Look for white wing bars—this is the only warbler, without distinct streaking on the back or underparts, that has them. There is also a pale eyebrow. The female is just a bit duller overall. Listen for the song, a soft and musical trill not unlike the chipping sparrow's (see page 142) but a little slower.

Palm Warbler

Dendroica palmarum

Chestnut-capped, tail-flicking warbler of palm woods in winter, muskeg bogs in summer.

The name "Palm warbler" fits this bird perfectly for part of the year—the wintering part, when it resides in Florida and along the Gulf Coast, preferring palm habitat. (Some birds winter in the palms of the West Indies and Honduras as well.) But once the palm warbler reaches its nesting grounds in central and northern Canada, it could almost have its name changed to "bog warbler" or "muskeg warbler." That is where the palm warbler will nest, in a place so far and different from its wintering habitat.

You can see a palm warbler most anywhere along its migration route, most often in weedy fields and near marsh edges. This warbler is a ground feeder, and this is rare among warblers. The scarce Kirtland's warbler is the only other ground-feeding species in the clan. Palm warblers nest on the ground as well.

A palm warbler is predominantly olive-colored, with yellow to creamy underparts that are only finely streaked. There is a handsome, chestnut-colored cap. The tail's under-coverts are bright yellow. The wings are not barred.

Watch for the bird's constantly wagging and flicking tail (always flicking upward), a trait unique to this particular warbler. That and its ground-feeding tendencies should tip you off to its identification. Males and females look very similar. Listen for the dry, buzzy song: a repititious trill.

American Redstart

Setophaga ruticilla

Flashes of orange in the woods.

For a bird so common in summer across much of the U.S., few people can claim to have ever seen many redstarts, or even one at all. The bird is named for its red-orange *start*, an Old English word meaning *tail*. That tail is seemingly always active: fanning and flashing the color. Redstarts do this color-flashing with their wings too, drooping and spreading them out to show off the bright orange patches. The bird is an active hunter, energetically flitting about as it snatches insects.

If a redstart sits still long enough for you to take a good look, here is what you'll see. The male is black on the head, back and chest, with a white belly. Most distinctive are the bright orange-red patches on his wings and tail; watch for the dropping and spreading displays described. Something unique among warblers: He looks the same in winter as in summer.

On the other hand, the female is olive-brown, with the same placement on her color patches, only they are more yellow than orange. Immature males look similar to females, and don't get their black-and-orange adult plumage until they are a full year old.

American redstarts love second-growth woodlands, and are willing nesters over much of the U.S. and Canada. The song is a couple of high-pitched phrases sounding like *see-see-see-see-seeo*, but varies with the locale.

Blackburnian Warbler

Dendroica fusca

Treetop dweller with a throat of flame.

This bright, sprightly bird is a jewel even among all the other colorful warblers that fill the spring woods. A male Blackburnian warbler looks almost like a fantasy bird a child might color … a throat of the most vivid orange possible, with stripes of the same fiery orange alternating with black on the head. The Blackburnian also wears a black facemask, and large white wing patches that contrast with the black that covers most of the rest of the body. The belly is streaked, and fades from orange to yellow to creamy. Females follow the same color pattern, but wear a paler orange or yellow.

Despite all this color, Blackburnian warblers are often hard to spot, because they like to stay high in the tree canopy where they acrobatically work the tips and twigs of branches on their hunt for bugs and caterpillars. One good way to locate them is to be out in the woods during the big spring warbler migration, from the end of April through mid-May or so as the birds head north to nesting grounds.

While you're out, listen for the male's high-pitched *slee-slee-slee-slee-slee* or *tidly-tidly-tidly-tidly* song, usually with the last note slurred and rising. Blackburnian warblers nest in mixed coniferous/deciduous forests through the Appalachians, across the Northeast, and westward across the northern tier of states all the way up into Saskatchewan.

Common Yellowthroat

Geothlypis trichas

Black-masked warbler of marshes, and thickets close to water.

*L*isten for the cheerful *witchity-witchity-witchity-witch* song of the common yellowthroat whenever you are near moist thickets, or wetlands with a brushy edge. If you do hear this bright and happy song, look for the bird in amongst the cover.

The male is bright yellow on the throat and upper breast, and has a bold black facemask that extends all the way down his neck; this mask is bordered with white. He is olive-brown above. Females and young males keep their namesake yellow throats, but lack the black mask, opting instead for the same olive-brown as the wings, tail and back.

If you hear a yellowthroat (either the loud song described or its harsh *chek* call) but can't see the bird, try luring it out where you can see it by making a lisping *pssh-pssh* sound. Sometimes this works on these energetic and curious birds.

This is another very common warbler that few people ever really see, even though yellowthroats nest across the United States wherever there are a few wet, marshy, brushy areas. Yellowthroats are worth looking for, so bold and handsome with their yellow and black accents.

Yellow-Breasted Chat

Icteria virens

*A very widepsread but shy and secretive warbler
of brush and thickets.*

The yellow-breasted chat is large for a warbler, at up to 7½ inches long, and there is some question as to whether it should really be classified as a warbler at all. A yellow-breasted chat really doesn't care—it just wants to be left alone in the thickets and shrubby tangles it calls home.

The song is odd, not like a warbler's, and it actually sounds more like a series of whistles alternating with mini, crow-like "caws." The bird loves to twitter and chatter, and the name "Chat" comes from that talkativeness. Some birders say the song is a little like a mockingbird's, and that is interesting because the chat will sing at night as well.

But for as chatty as a chat can be, finding one can be hard because they stick to thick cover—thorny, dense thickets are favorite places, especially if there is some water nearby.

When you combine "chat" with "yellow-breasted," the name gives a very accurate and complete description of the bird. Look for the yellow throat and breast, and the white belly. The bird is olive-green above, and there is a white patch in front of the eye, a white eye ring, and a small patch of black below the eye. Hear the chattering too? There you have it—a yellow-breasted chat.

A Gallery of Warblers

The warblers on the previous pages represent some of the more common yard and garden visitors you might see. But there's actually a whole world of warblers out there, waiting for you to discover it. Here are some of the other members of this colorful bird family.

Nashville Warbler

Vermivora ruficapilla

Orange-Crowned Warbler

Vermivora celata

Bay-Breasted Warbler

Dendroica castanea

Blackpoll Warbler

Dendroica striata

Tennessee Warbler

Vermivora peregrina

Cape May Warbler

Dendroica tigrina

Cerulean Warbler

Dendroica cerulea

Northern Parula

Parula americana

Black-Throated Blue Warbler

Dendroica caerulescens

Worm-Eating Warbler

Helmitheros vermivorus

Yellow-Throated Warbler

Dendroica dominica

Hooded Warbler

Wilsonia citrina

Prairie Warbler

Dendroica discolor

Black-Throated Green Warbler

Dendroica virens

Prothonotary Warbler

Protonotaria citrea

Canada Warbler

Wilsonia canadensis

Woodpeckers

Woodpeckers don't ask for much (a couple of old trees, a little cover, some seeds, a little bit of suet), but they provide lively color, plenty of activity and even sound in return. Okay, so the rat-tat-tat-tat of a woodpecker can grow on your nerves a little bit at 5:30 a.m. But it's just another being making its living. And if you are able to attract some of these woodpeckers, Nature would surely agree that you're doing something right in your garden.

From a tiny downy woodpecker to a giant pileated, these insect- and larvae-eaters provide important (and free) pest control services, in addition to their contributions of sound, energy and color.

Downy Woodpecker

Picoides pubescens

Our smallest woodpecker, a friendly and willing visitor to yards, gardens and feeders.

You can find downy woodpeckers almost anywhere across the U.S. and Canada, wherever there are trees: woodlots (deciduous or coniferous), treed riverbottoms out on the plains, yards, parks and gardens.

Typical of woodpeckers, the downy loves eating insects more than anything else. A downy will work its way up a tree, probing the bark's cracks and crevices as it goes. Two wonderful features aid the downy in this quest: a stiff tail the bird uses as a prop as it pecks, prods, pokes and probes; and four toes on each foot, two of which face forward and two backward. These toes improve the bird's grip and maneuvering ability during its acrobatic insect hunt. The tongue is extra long, and barbed, to help in probing for, as well as catching and extracting, prey.

In summer, the downy concentrates almost exclusively on insect food. In winter, the ratio of vegetable matter (seeds, nuts, dried fruit) in the diet rises, but suet or other fat is still the best attractor (see tip). Sunflower seeds do a good job attracting downies as well.

TIP: Downies love suet. Feed it in a bag, or in one of the popular suet baskets. It's fun to watch an acrobatic downy work over the suet; a hanging basket may help discourage starlings.

The downy is a wonderful bird for the garden and feeders because it is not especially nervous, will visit often, and can become quite tame to your presence. In winter, downies are common members of the mixed-flock battalions of chickadees-nuthatches-titmice-creepers-woodpeckers that patrol countryside and townscape.

IDENTIFICATION

The downy woodpecker's tail takes up a good chunk of its 6-inch length, so this really is a small bird … approximately sparrow-sized but much leaner. A downy is downright handsome with black wings spotted with white, a mostly white back, and a black head with two white stripes. One of these stripes passes just through and above the eye, the other from the bill to cheek. The male sports a red patch on the nape (back of the head). The call is a descending, rattling slur of notes. There is also a one-note *pik* call.

NESTING

The downy woodpecker is a cavity nester. To start, the male will establish a territory, and drum on all manner of limbs, trees, buildings, telephone poles, aluminum siding—almost anything—to advertise and define his turf. Both male and female will work together to excavate a hole in an old tree or rotten portion of any tree, making sure to leave some wood chips behind for making a soft bed for the nest cup. There the female will lay 4–5 white eggs; both she and the male will share incubation duties until the chicks hatch in 12 days. The youngsters fledge 21–24 days after that.

TIP: Leave dead trees and snags up in your yard and garden, as long as possible until personal or property safety becomes a concern. Downy woodpeckers and a host of other birds will love the opportunity for food and nesting sites. The color and joy they will bring to your yard far outweigh the thought of leaving a dead tree around. You could hang a nest box too; a hole 1⅜ inches in diameter should be sufficient.

TIP: As for seeds, downy woodpeckers like sunflower best. If you can afford hulled seeds, all the better.

TIP: Differentiating between downy and hairy woodpeckers (pages 130-131) can be confusing because their plumage is essentially the same. The best way to learn the difference is to get lucky and see them side-by-side one time, being observant to study how much bigger a hairy is. His bill is very long and stout compared to the downy's relatively tiny one. A good rule of thumb: If you can easily see the bill, it's a hairy. Also, the downy's call is more of a *pik* versus the hairy's *peek*.

▶ Inset: Female downy woodpecker.

Hairy Woodpecker

Picoides villosus

Larger cousin of the downy woodpecker, with its own unique personality and habits.

The hairy and the downy woodpecker look about the same, and have similar life strategies. But the hairy is a third again as big. And if anything, the hairy's range is larger than the downy's. So how can the two coexist?

For starters, hairies seem to prefer bigger forests and more isolated areas, which keeps the two species working different trees for the ants, aphids, beetles, larvae and other insect matter they love to eat. Even when the species are found together, the hairy's much larger, stronger and longer bill—coupled with his incredibly long (twice as long as his bill) barbed tongue—allows him to forage successfully even where a downy has already been. This is because he can go deeper into bark crevices, after pounding away a deeper hole with his big bill. He is just bigger, stronger and more powerful, and can work deeper.

Like other woodpeckers, the hairy has two forward-facing toes and two backward-facing ones, for clinging to and moving about trees.

Though shy and reclusive compared to the downy, a hairy woodpecker still willingly visits feeders for suet and seeds (see attracting tips). Hairy woodpeckers serve gardeners well by eating large volumes of harmful beetles and other wood-boring insect pests, and eating the larvae of other insects.

In addition to all the insect life, larvae and grubs it consumes, a hairy woodpecker will eat a variety of seeds (acorns, corn and walnuts, peanuts and sunflower at the feeder), fruits in season (mulberries, serviceberries, apples, chokecherries, poison ivy) and other sources of fat such as deer or other carcasses in the woods.

TIP: Hang out a suet feeder to attract hairy woodpeckers.

TIP: If you have a hunter in the family or know one, and they butcher their own deer, ask them to save the rib cage or some leg bones. Hang one or the other from a tree limb when winter starts, and it will keep the hairies—and other woodpeckers as well—very happy as they work it over for the attached meat and fat. Replace the carcass part with another piece after the birds have stripped it.

IDENTIFICATION

Basically, a hairy woodpecker looks just like a downy except that he is larger: robin-sized at 9 inches in length, but slender. Look for the white back, black wings spotted with white, white facial stripes, and the small red patch on the back of the male's head. A hairy's bill is much larger—readily visible with the naked eye even at a distance; this is a good identification giveaway. But as you get familiar with the hairy, you will know at a glance it is him just by the sheer size compared to the little downy; this is an impressive and very good-looking bird. The hairy's call is louder, and is more of a *peek* versus the downy's *pik*.

NESTING

Hairy woodpeckers nest in tree holes, the male and female working to excavate a 10- to 12-inch-deep cavity with their powerful bills. This cavity is anywhere from 5 to 40 feet above the ground. The female will lay 3–4 white eggs and incubate them by day, with the male taking over at night. The young hatch after 2 weeks, and then keep both parents incredibly busy feeding the gaping mouths until fledging takes place in 28–30 days. Note the relatively long fledging time; the hairy is a bigger woodpecker, and it takes longer for the youngsters to grow big enough to leave the nest.

TIP: Peanuts will keep hairy woodpeckers coming back to your feeding station. The big-billed birds seem to handle the large, tough peanuts well. A good way to offer them is shelled, in a basket the woodpecker can cling to.

▶ Inset: Female hairy woodpecker.

Red-Bellied Woodpecker

Melanerpes carolinus

Not so red-bellied after all.

This gorgeous woodpecker, usually thought of as a Southerner, has steadily expanded its range northward over the last century. The name *red-bellied* is a sort of oddity, because you can really only see a wash of red on the mostly buff belly if you are close and the light is perfect. The distinguishing feature is the scarlet headpatch, which starts on the nape and, on the male, runs clear to the bill's base (see photo). In certain locales, a red-belly is known as a "zebraback" because of the barred black-and-white back and wings. The rump is white. Listen for the *chuck-chuck-chuck* or single *kwirrrr* call.

The red-bellied woodpecker includes more seeds and fruits in its diet than other woodpeckers do, and loves acorns, beechnuts, hickory nuts, and fruits and berries of all descriptions. Stashing foods like this—most often in crevices in bark—prepares this woodpecker for lean times. The red-belly does its share in reducing insect, beetle, cricket and grasshopper populations as well.

TIP: Red-bellied woodpeckers will readily come to corn. Leave it on a tree feeder, or nail an ear to a tree or stump. If you have some walnuts around, crack them in half and leave them out for red-bellies to pull out the meats. As with other woodpeckers, a red-belly won't pass up suet either.

Yellow-Bellied Sapsucker

Sphyrapicus varius

Specializing in sap.

This woodpecker is named for its very specialized feeding habit. It will bore rows of holes in a tree's bark, let the sap ooze into the holes, then lap up the sap with its long, brush-like tongue. This is a major food source for the sapsucker, and the holes provide benefits to other wildlife as well: hummingbirds, nuthatches, warblers, squirrels and insects are also attracted to the sap. A sapsucker will return again and again to holes it has made, picking up the insects that keep coming to the sweet "bait" as a bonus.

The belly isn't as bright as one might think from the bird's name, but is a dull yellow. More prominent are the male's and female's red crown, and the male's red (female's white) throat patch. The back is mottled brown and black. A good identifier: both male and female yellow-bellieds have a distinctive white wing patch that you can see when the bird is both in flight and at rest. The bird shown at right is a female.

The yellow-bellied sapsucker nests across the northern states and into Canada, and migrates southward in winter. The related red-naped sapsucker lives in the Rocky Mountains.

TIP: Rows of holes indicate a sapsucker has been at work. They are not picky at the species of tree or shrub they use, and over 275 have been identified as sap sources. (Shown above: Red-naped sapsucker, a western relative of the yellow-belly.)

Pileated Woodpecker

Dryocopus pileatus

Impressive, elegant and elusive all at once: Our largest woodpecker.

At first sighting, a pileated woodpecker is almost unbelievable: a spectacular, mostly black bird with white neck stripes, white linings on the undersides of the wings (the white is highly visible when the bird is in flight), and a stunning, flaming-red crest. Overall, it's about the size of a crow! And that beak—so large and heavy you *know* it can inflict some major holes into a tree.

Then again, you might hear a pileated woodpecker working a tree in the woods, and wonder what kind of mutant downy or hairy woodpecker could make a loud, resounding racket like that. Even the call—a loud, ringing and deep *cuck-cuck-cuckcuck*—demands attention.

With all these impressive characteristics, you would think a pileated woodpecker would be easy to see. While they are more common than most people think, pileateds are birds of the forest. That love of deep forest makes them elusive, although they seem to have adapted well to wooded residential areas. Hardwoods are favored habitat and the larger the expanse the better, but even small groves, or lightly wooded areas along rivers or lakes or streets, will hold pileated woodpeckers.

TIP: Pileated woodpeckers reside in hardwood forests. The larger the expanse the better, but the birds seem to be doing increasingly well in residential areas that have mature trees.

But sometimes the only evidence of a pileated woodpecker's presence is the gaping hole—often rectangular in shape—left in soft or rotten wood in the course of the big woodpecker's search for ants, spiders, insect larvae and other insect matter. But keep your eyes and ears open, and sooner or later you will hear, and then maybe have to stalk to see, this most impressive of North American woodpeckers.

TIP: Pileated woodpeckers love suet, and can go through a lot of it. Because the birds are so large, they need a solid perch to cling to. So attach a suet basket directly and solidly to a tree or post.

IDENTIFICATION

As discussed at left, this woodpecker is *big* (crow-sized at 17 to 19 inches in length) and handsome in its plumage of black and white, with fiery-red crest on top of the head. To tell a male from a female, look at the forehead and "mustache" area to the side of the mouth. A female will have a black forehead (but still a red crest), and she will *not* have a red mustache (hers will be black compared to the male's red one). Look for the pileated's unique flap-and-glide flying technique, which could not be deemed graceful. The call is described at left.

NESTING

Pileated woodpecker pairs excavate a hole sized appropriately for a bird of these proportions; the tree must be at least 16 inches in diameter, in some stage of decay, and the cavity when finished will be at least 18 inches deep. Four to six white eggs are incubated for 18 days, and fledging takes place 5–6 weeks after that. (That's a long time—the parents work hard to keep the nestlings fed.)

Pileated woodpeckers will also dig cavities close to the nest, as alternate sleeping chambers for one parent or the other during nesting and rearing of the young. Quarters get tight in the main nesting cavity! All these cavities provide important future nesting opportunities for other birds, as well as tree squirrels, flying squirrels, raccoons and opossums.

▶ Shown: Female pileated woodpecker.

▶ Inset: Note the red mustache on the male pileated woodpecker.

Common Flicker

Colaptes auratus

Ant-eating woodpecker of the ground.

The common flicker is the only North American woodpecker that prefers to feed on the ground. It seems odd to see what is obviously a woodpecker fly down, land on the ground and start hunting for insects, but that is the niche this flicker has specialized into.

The animal world offers a mammal called "anteater," and the flicker is the bird world's closest counterpart. Perfectly suited for the task is the flicker's tongue: Three inches longer than the bill, it probes easily for ants (the primary and preferred food source) as well as beetles, caterpillars, crickets, grasshoppers, insect larvae … anything that crawls on the ground or within a couple inches of its surface. One study found over 5,000 ants in one flicker stomach! A flicker's diet consists of about 90% of this type of animal food in summer, when it is most available; about 40% of the winter diet is animal food.

Although they don't migrate any farther than they have to, flickers will move south in winter to find unfrozen ground. Other food includes fruit, from dogwood and blackberries to chokecherries and plums in season, as well as acorns, ragweed, corn, wheat, oats and other grain.

Flickers used to frequent yards across our country in summer, but are not as common any more, for several reasons. Heavy pesticide use has decreased or eliminated much of the flicker's insect prey. Invasive starlings take over their cavity nests. And our penchant for neatness and order has gotten rid of the older trees flickers need for nesting. As gardeners, we can do something about the first and third problems.

TIP: Flickers feed on the ground. One way you can help them: Avoid using pesticides that will kill their food sources and poison the insects that survive through the application.

TIP: Flickers will use a nest box. It has to be fairly large, to accommodate the parents and young, with an entrance hole 2½ inches in diameter 15 inches off the house's floor.

TIP: Flickers will come to suet feeders, peanut butter, or apples and raisins at a feeder.

TIP: The yellow-shafted flicker resides east of the Great Plains; the red-shafted west. These names come from the color of the birds' feather shafts, which give it a yellowish (East) or salmon-colored (West) cast from underneath, when the bird is in flight. Where the ranges overlap, the two freely interbreed, so they are considered one species. East or West, identify a male flicker by its mustache, which is black in the East and red in the West.

IDENTIFICATION

The flicker is named for its call: a loud, squeaky *flicker flicker flicker* or *wicka-wicka-wicka*. A couple of colloquial names, including wickup and yawker bird, reflect this voice. About 12 inches long, the flicker has a brown back that is barred with black, a creamy tan chest and belly (both spotted with black) and a white rump that flashes during the bird's undulating flight. In the East, a flicker will have a red patch on the nape.

NESTING

Like other members of the woodpecker family, a male flicker will hammer on trees, power poles, buildings, roofs, almost anything, to advertise his territory. He and the female will excavate a cavity anywhere from 3 to 60 feet up in a tree, where she will lay 3–6 white eggs. The female incubates the eggs by day, the male by night, until they hatch in 11–12 days. The young fledge after 25–28 days more.

Native Sparrows

To many bird lovers, "sparrow" is a dirty word, and that image does have merit when you're talking about imported, invasive house sparrows (actually members of the weaver finch family) that have caused the decline of a wide variety of native bird species. But here, we're talking about native sparrows, true sparrows—birds of the forest, savannah and grassland that have inhabited North America since time immemorial.

Fortunately, many of these native sparrows have adapted well to man's use of the land, and we can still take comfort in their beautiful songs and colors-of-the-wild.

Song Sparrow

Melospiza melodia

A birdfeeder favorite, common across North America.

The song sparrow is probably North America's most successful native sparrow, with 31 distinct subspecies identified to date. These variations range from the large (over 7 inches), dark and long-billed song sparrow of the Aleutian Islands, to tiny, pale birds of the desert Southwest.

Even though song sparrows are common, they are interesting birds—beautiful in their own right, both in their looks and in their singing. Even the Latin species name, *melodia*, recognizes this. The song sparrow's is one of the first beautiful songs to be heard as winter starts giving way to spring. Audubon described the song as *Maids-Maids-Maids hang-up-your-tea-kettle-ettle-ettle.* But there are many variations to this tune. And if you listen closely, you can even begin to identify individual birds by their own particular melody. It is truly a song of summer, although it can actually be heard any time of year.

Song sparrows inhabit thickets, overgrown pastures, forest openings and backyards. They like farmland, especially fields interspersed with plenty of brushy fencerows and woodlots and wetlands. The birds scratch for food on the ground—primarily seeds such as grass seeds of all kinds, cracked corn, millet, oats, wheat, sunflower, ragweed, foxtail and more. Plant food makes up about 60% of the diet in summer (when many insects, caterpillars, crickets and grasshoppers are also taken to help feed the nestlings) and 90% in winter.

Some song sparrows move southward to escape the brunt of winter, not to tropical places but at least a province or a couple of states south. But many song sparrows will winter right in their year-round range, in the central states, and some will overwinter close to home as far north as the states touching the Canadian border. At this and other times of year, the song sparrow is a willing visitor to feeders, another reason for its place in the hearts of many bird lovers.

TIP: The song sparrow may not be our most beautiful native sparrow, but its singing is unmatched—full of joy and good cheer.

TIP: Song sparrows willingly visit feeders. Millet, cracked corn or bread crumbs on the ground do a good job. The birds will also glean sunflower and other seeds dropped from your regular tray feeders. If you have song sparrows staying the winter, don't forget them when it snows. Keep a ground feeding tray open for them and stock it with fresh seed; or just spread new, accessible seed or crumbs on the ground.

IDENTIFICATION

Although appearance varies across its range, here is a general description of the song sparrow: A 5½- to 7-inch-long bird with faintly-streaked, reddish brown upper parts and lighter, heavily-streaked underparts. The underparts' streaks meet in a spot in the middle of the breast. That spot is a very important field identification mark. A gray stripe sits atop the eye (this is a good field mark too). Song sparrows pump their tails as they fly—watch for this as well. Listen for the lovely song (described at left) as well as the *tseet* or *chep* calls given by members of a flock as they forage in the brush.

NESTING

Song sparrows try to raise as many broods as possible in a season, sometimes bringing 3 off before autumn. The first nest may be on the ground, but once the leaves are out, the birds will attempt to hatch a family low in a shrub or small conifer—only 1 to 4 feet off the ground. The nest cup is made of grass strips, weed stems, rootlets and leaves, sometimes lined with hair or feathers. The female lays 3–6 light green eggs spotted with brown, and incubates them for 12–13 days. It takes only 10 more for the young to fledge and soon they're on their own so that the parents can get busy with another brood, if enough summer remains.

TIP: A key field identification tip: Look for the spot on the song sparrow's streaked breast.

Chipping Sparrow

Spizella passerina

Tiny, rusty-capped sparrow of yards and gardens.

Chipping sparrows have almost certainly benefited from all of man's activities on the land.

These friendly, attractive little sparrows thrive in city and suburban yards, gardens and parks, as well as brushy pastures. They love brushy cover to escape to, but spend most of their time foraging on the ground and in the open for weed seeds, grass seeds and insects; here, they can easily be enjoyed and admired. These habitats were certainly less common a couple centuries ago.

And as you'll see in the nesting section, when horses were the preferred mode of human transportation, chipping sparrows used that equine hair to line their nests. Of course now chippers utilize other hair for their nests (and in fact are sometimes colloquially known as *hairbird*). But most chipping sparrows around today probably descend, somewhere along the line, from ancestors hatched on horsehair.

Chipping sparrows range broadly, nesting across the U.S. from east to west and north to south, on up through Canada to the Arctic Circle. Birds from the Far North will travel only as far south as needed in winter, to escape snow-covered ground and find places where they can forage; birds nesting farther south, in the central states, will retreat southward as well, conveniently making room for the northern migrants.

TIP: Chipping sparrows love evergreens of any type for nesting cover. Spruces seem to be a favorite, but yew is popular too. Be careful of nests when trimming your shrubs.

Chipping sparrows are confirmed seed and plant material eaters (90% of their diet in the colder months), but feed on insects fairly heavily (50% of their diet in summer) to give young chicks a high-protein jump-start. Chipping sparrows are not known to eat fruit.

There's nothing quite like hearing the happy trilling of a chipping sparrow out on the yard or garden, then looking out to see the little red-capped visitor hopping about.

TIP: How to tell a chipping sparrow from a tree sparrow: a chipping sparrow will *not* have a dark spot on its breast.

IDENTIFICATION

A tiny (only 5 to 5½ inches) sparrow that is streaked brown above and solid gray below. There is a black line through the eye, a white line above the eye, and a prominent chestnut-colored cap (that could also be described as orange-red, rusty-red or rufous … take your pick); these are all important identification marks. Males and females look alike. In winter, the cap and eyebrow line get duller. Listen for the song, a high-pitched and rattly trill. Although chipping sparrows stay on or near the ground most of the time, they will sing from perches during nesting season. The call gives the chipping sparrow its name—a simple, dry-sounding *chip* given as it forages on the ground.

NESTING

Chipping sparrows seem to like human company, and will readily nest near buildings. A favorite spot is within foundation plantings of coniferous shrubs, especially spruces. Shrubbery and tangles of vines, low to the ground, are also good spots. The nest, a tiny cup, is made of grass and stems; in times past, when horses were the world's primary mode of transportation, chipping sparrow nests were almost invariably lined with horsehair. In this hair-lined nest the female lays 3–5 pale blue or blue-green eggs that she incubates for 11–14 days. The young fledge quickly, only 8–12 days after that. The parents will attempt two broods in a summer.

TIP: Red and white millet, spread on the ground, will attract chipping sparrows to your yard; so will the seeds of all types—especially sunflower and niger thistle—that fall to the ground from your hanging feeders.

American Tree Sparrow

Spizella arborea

An odd name for a bird that spends so little time in trees.

How the American tree sparrow got its name is anyone's guess, for over its lifetime this handsome little bird will spend less time in a real, mature tree than almost any other bird.

This is a northern sparrow, a summer resident and nester on the open plains just south of the Arctic tundra in Alaska, the Northwest Territories and across the top of Canada. Tree sparrows visit the U.S.—chiefly the northern two-thirds of the country—in winter. At this time you can see big flocks (sometimes up to 40 or 50 birds) working the countryside and backyards.

Favored habitat at this time of year includes hedgerows, brushy edges, marshes, roadside thickets and backyards with some low, woody cover nearby … somewhere with plenty of open fields and expanses where the birds can forage on the ground for weed and grass seeds. Tree sparrow winter habitat fairly well replicates the tundra plains with dwarf brush that the tree sparrow summers and nests in—scrubby thickets of birch, alder and spruce with many openings.

One interesting feeding adaptation: a tree sparrow will hover around a seed pod, flapping its wings against the pod to scatter some seeds to the snow-covered ground; then the bird will drop down to pick up the harvest. Tree sparrows primarily eat seeds, but will also take insects (especially when nesting) and fruit in season.

Tree sparrows are willing and faithful wintertime feeder visitors, and seem to appreciate the handout (see tips) after their long trip south. Look for tree sparrows between November-December and March-April depending on your latitude. Whether they come in any given year depends a lot on the winter weather—the harsher it is in the Far North, the more tree sparrows seem to come south.

TIP: American tree sparrows will visit your winter feeder, preferring to stay on or near the ground. Try a feeding tray with white millet or hulled sunflower. Tree sparrows will also gladly glean what falls to the ground from your hanging feeders.

TIP: Tree sparrows are actually birds of the open, preferring scrubby thickets, lowland brush and open fields, meadows and gardens, over mature trees and forest.

IDENTIFICATION

An American tree sparrow is streaked brown/chestnut above and solid gray below, with a rusty/chestnut cap on a gray head. A stripe through the eye is the same rusty/chestnut color as the cap. Look for the dark blotch on the breast, and a bill that is dark on top and yellow below. Although a bit larger than the chipping sparrow, the tree sparrow still only averages 6 inches or so in length. Look for the blotch on the chest, two-toned bill and the two white wing bars, to distinguish the tree sparrow from the similar chipping sparrow. The tree sparrow's voice: birds feeding together give a musical *see-ler* or *tsee* call. A courting males sings several high notes followed by some trilling warbles, but you'll have to be up on the tundra to hear that.

NESTING

Strangely enough, tree sparrows nest low in scrubby tundra bushes, or right on the ground. The nest is made of grass pieces, weed stems and bark strips lined with hair, feathers and fur the parents can find. This well-insulated cup houses 4–5 pale blue, brown-speckled eggs as the female incubates them for 12–13 days. The fledglings leave the nest after only 10 days, but it takes them 3 or 4 more to learn to fly. In the short arctic summer, only one brood is possible.

TIP: For positive identification of a tree sparrow, look for the unstreaked gray breast with brown blotch, two-colored bill (dark on top and yellowish below), two white wing bars and a rusty-chestnut stripe through the eye.

White-Throated Sparrow

Zonotrichia albicollis

Gorgeous song of spring.

For many bird lovers one sound, more than any other, indicates winter has truly broken and spring is here for good: the song of the white-throated sparrow. It would be hard to find a happier, more pleasant song at any time of year: a melody of clear, whistling notes that has been described as *Poor Sam Peabody Peabody Peabody* or *Sweet Pure Canada Canada Canada.*

The latter rendition names the white-throated sparrow's primary breeding range—the coniferous woodlands of Canada from Labrador, Quebec and Newfoundland all the way across to Saskatchewan, Alberta and the Northwest Territories. Some birds nest in New England, northern Minnesota, Wisconsin and Michigan.

White-throats winter in the southern United States, and as far south as Mexico. It is during the migration northward in spring, and southward in fall, that we usually get to see this attractive sparrow. October-November and March-April are the best times to locate one in your yard or garden.

White-throats seem to be wintering farther and farther north, probably a function of their willingness to come to bird feeders. White-throats will spend the winter in yards and gardens, brushy woodlands and overgrown pastures.

In addition to the supplemental winter food helping them survive the harsh winters, being farther north at the start of migration makes the entire spring trip less strenuous for white-throated sparrows, and they're in better shape to take on nesting duties. With the hardier birds at this nesting advantage, they are the ones producing more white-throats to replace them— white-throats that will also tend to winter farther north.

Like many other sparrows, the white-throat eats predominantly weed seeds in spring, fall and winter, although in summer it will take 50% insects in its diet, to help feed the nestlings, as well as fruits and berries as they ripen.

TIP: To positively identify a white-throated sparrow, look for the well-defined white throat patch (versus a gray throat on a white-crowned sparrow), and the yellow spot between the eye and beak.

TIP: The white-throated sparrow arguably sings the bird world's most beautiful, lilting springtime song. Stop to enjoy it.

IDENTIFICATION

This 6-to-7-inch-long sparrow is rusty-brown above and gray below, with a prominent white throat patch, black-and-white-striped head and a distinctive yellow spot in front of the eye. This is the bird you will see during the spring migration. The stripes on some white-throats' heads are not so contrasting and more of a black-tan than black-white, but they are still the same species; this describes winter birds as well—a bit duller overall, not quite as striking. The beautiful song, described at left, heralds spring. The call is somewhat harsh and sounds like *pink*, *tink* or *tseet*; listen for this in the underbrush.

NESTING

White-throated sparrows nest on or near the ground, building a cup of twigs, grasses and moss. Sometimes this cozy nest is even placed under a brushpile for overhead cover. There the female lays 4 pale green, brown-speckled eggs that she incubates for 12–14 days. Fledging takes 7–12 days more. At best, parents can pull off only one brood in the short, northern summer.

TIP: Spread seed on the ground to attract white-throats. White proso millet and cracked corn are welcomed during the migration periods. If you have white-throats wintering near you, be sure to spread seed after a snowfall: something the tiny sparrows can get at. These birds are tough, but can only go so deep in scratching away snow cover from their food sources. Platform feeders will also serve white-throats.

White-Crowned Sparrow

Zonotrichia leucophrys

A *native sparrow of the Far North, as well as Western Mountains.*

*I*t is unfortunate that the name "sparrow" carries so much baggage with it. This stems mostly from the negative feelings surrounding the aggressive and invasive house sparrow, which was introduced from Europe to North America and is really not a sparrow at all but a weaver finch. And this is unfortunate, because there are so many interesting, true and native sparrows to know and admire, and this is another in the line-up.

The white-crowned sparrow is a boreal bird like its white-throated cousin, nesting across the northern regions of Canada. But westerners are graced with white crowns as well, as the bird also nests in Rocky Mountain fir forests from Canada all the way down to Colorado, New Mexico and Arizona. White-crowned sparrows of the Far North will travel southward for winter, while mountain birds will descend in elevation. White-crowned sparrow migration patterns have been heavily studied by researchers and biologists, and white-crowns serve as a sort of example species in trying to determine general migration strategies.

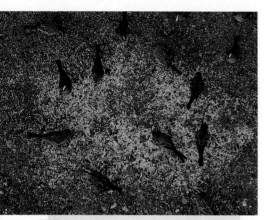

TIP: Unless you spend summers in the Far North, or way up in the alpine West, migration is the time to see white-crowned sparrows. Scatter millet, sunflower seeds and cracked grain to attract them from March through early May, and then again from September through early December.

The white-crown is a handsome sparrow that looks very similar to a white-throated sparrow (see identification notes), but is not as commonly sighted. It seems to be more of a bird of the wilderness and outback. Migration time is the best time to see a white-crown. Sometimes, if you let your eyes search carefully through a flock of white-throats, you can spy a white-crown or two in the bunch.

White-crowns forage on the ground for small seeds of all kinds. Insect matter creeps into the diet in summer—ants, grasshoppers, crickets, spiders, beetles and the like—when chick-raising duties are in full swing.

TIP: The white-crown likes to have open areas around—these spots usually produce good weed harvests as well as insects—but the bird requires some shrubby or wooded areas for cover. They will migrate right through your yard and garden, so be watchful.

IDENTIFICATION

This 6½- to 7½-inch-long sparrow looks much like a white-throated sparrow. The upper parts are streaked brown, the lower parts a clear and pretty gray. There is one broad stripe down the center of the head, with a black stripe flanking either side of it, then another set of white stripes going through the eye to the back of the head. The bill is pinkish, and there is no white throat patch as in the white-throated sparrow. Another distinguishing feature: the white-crown does not have a yellow spot between its eyes and beak. The white-crown's song is not quite as melodious as the white-throat's, but is still a lovely series of notes and trills.

NESTING

White-crowns nest in the brush, on the ground or very near it in a low fork or branch of a shrub. The nest is made of bark strips and twigs, and lined with grass and hair. The female lays 4 or 5 pale green eggs that are spotted with brown, and incubates them for 12 days. The young white-crowns fledge only 12 days after that, and soon are on their own for the most part, although they will stick with the family group through migration and the winter months, until it's time to return to scrubby boreal forest or mountain slopes and nest on their own.

TIP: Look for the pinkish bill to be sure it is a white-crowned sparrow you're looking at. No yellow spot between the eyes and beak is another indication that it is a white-crown and not a white-throat.

Fox Sparrow

Passerella iliaca

A large sparrow of forest and brush, colored like a red fox.

The widespread fox sparrow lives in the thick coniferous forests of the North and West all summer, from Alaska across the top of Canada, as well as down either side of the Rocky Mountains' spine. In autumn, fox sparrows migrate southward and to lower elevations, where they winter in dense woodland underbrush, thickets, fencerows and brushy, overgrown pastures.

TIP: The fox sparrow is a ground feeder. Listen for the thrashing about of leaves and other forest floor debris as the bird hops about and scratches in its search for seeds and insects.

The fall migration, and again in the spring when birds are moving back northward or upward, is the best time to see a fox sparrow. Look for a large bird—larger than you think a sparrow should be—on the ground. The predominant color is a bright, rufous, rusty red not unlike that of a red fox (hence the source of the fox sparrow's name). These factors make a fox sparrow fairly easily distinguishable from other sparrows. See identification notes at right, as well.

It is a handsome and very successful bird, and 18 different "looks" have been identified across its range. For instance, western fox sparrows are more brown and even gray than their eastern counterparts, reflecting the more arid climate. Birds in the Pacific Northwest are very dark around the head, a function of their moist, humid habitat.

The fox sparrow feeds primarily on the ground, and has the interesting habit of hopping along backward and forward, kicking up leaves to uncover seeds and insects below, just like a towhee. Fortunately, in the fox sparrow's wintering grounds, the towhees have migrated southward by the time fox sparrows move in, so the two don't compete in the brushy undergrowth they prefer. One fox sparrow can make a lot of noise doing this, more than you would think from one relatively small bird.

IDENTIFICATION

At 6¾ to 7½ inches long, this is a large sparrow in the scheme of things. This, along with the bright, rusty coloration of the tail (which is very conspicuous in flight), wings and back, sets this sparrow apart from others. The white underparts display heavy, rufous streaking, and there is one rufous-red blotch in the center of the bird's chest. The head and neck are gray, with reddish stripes. The bill is heavy, darker on top and lighter below. The song is nice; a loud and short but sweet warble.

NESTING

Fox sparrows prefer nesting in coniferous forests, where they build a thick-walled nest of moss, twigs and grass. Like other native sparrows' nests, this nest is on or close to the ground. The female lays 4–5 eggs that are pale green and marked with reddish brown, and incubates them for 12–14 days. The young fledge 10 days after that.

▶ Fox sparrows take on many different looks, but they are all of one species. This bird is from Pennsylvania.

TIP: For most gardeners, migration is the time you can see a fox sparrow, although the birds winter across the southern states, and at lower elevations in the West.

Rufous-Sided Towhee

Pipilo erythrophthalmus

A handsome bird of the underbrush, named for its distinctive to-whee call.

The best place to see a towhee is in thickets and brushy woodland edges, where the bird hunts for spiders, ants, beetles, snails, crickets, moths and insects of every description. The hunting method is unique, and observing it is good confirmation that you really are looking at a towhee: the bird will jump forward and then backward, exposing the bare ground below the leaves and duff—and insect prey scurrying for cover.

Towhees are handsome birds, members of our family of native sparrows (see identification notes for the basics) with an interesting twist: Both eastern and western forms were once thought to be separate species. But, as is the case with so many songbirds, when East meets West in the plains and prairies, the two freely interbreed. All towhees are now known as just rufous-sided towhee. The eastern form used to be called the red-eyed towhee; the western form, the spotted towhee. Towhees in Florida and the Southeast often have white eyes; this contrasts with the usual red.

In addition to insects, towhees will eat berries and seeds in season, once the food has fallen to the ground. The list of favorite foods is long and includes blackberries, grapes, raspberries, plums, ragweed, acorns and hickory nuts. Notice that all these are products of woodlands and dense cover. Towhees love thick cover, even brushpiles, with deciduous trees overhead. Listen for their noisy scratching as they work the forest floor. Oak woodlands are a favored habitat.

TIP: Towhees stay under cover in their hopping, kick-and-jump hunt for insects, berries and seeds.

IDENTIFICATION

In the East, a male towhee displays bright rufous (robin-colored) sides, a black head and back, white belly, and vibrant red eyes. White patches on the wings and tail flash in flight. Add white spots to the back and wings and you have a western male. Females are similar to males East and West, but brown replaces the black. The call gives this bird its name, a clear *to-whee* which could also be interpreted as *chew-ink*. The song is pretty, a wavering *drink-yer-teeee*. Towhees reach from 7 to 9 inches in length, so are sized like a robin but aren't quite as plump. Towhees are related to our native sparrows.

NESTING

The female builds the nest of twigs, leaves and bark shreds low to the ground in a shrub or vine, possibly even right on the ground. The surrounding cover is always dense. There she lays 3–4 creamy-colored eggs that are spotted with brown. She incubates them for 12 days, and the young fledge 10–12 days after that.

TIP: Cutting some brush? Leave a brushpile as towhee cover, if you have some woods or an odd, brushy corner in your yard. You could also scatter some shelled corn, crushed crackers, peanut meats, sunflower heart or even watermelon seeds on the ground, just outside of some cover, to lure towhees into view.

Swallows & Flycatchers

Swooping, swerving, diving, dodging, darting, looping . . . there are almost endless ways to describe a swallow's flight as it hunts down insects. Sometimes this flight is so fast, it's hard to get a good look and see just how beautiful the bird really is. On the other hand, flycatchers often perch or hover as they wait for prey, and you can get a good look from the start.

These are birds that readily take to yards and gardens if you know what to offer, and they help you control—at least a little bit—that crop of insects that always seems to come with warm weather.

Barn Swallow

Hirundo rustica

Graceful, split-tailed swallow of buildings and waterways.

*S*ome people dislike barn swallows for their penchant for building mud-cup nests on manmade structures of all kinds: under the eaves of barns, houses or outbuildings; on girders and rafters; and under, on and around bridges. But who can blame the swallows? All these spots make perfect, protected nesting nooks—far better than the caves, cliffs and stream banks barn swallows used to have to find. They seldom use these natural places any more.

But, fortunately, more people love barn swallows—for their grace, beauty and insect-eating capabilities. These are among the first birds to appear with warm weather as spring advances northward; some birds winter as far south as Argentina. As soon as there are insects around, the swallows will be close behind, both literally and figuratively. Lakes and rivers are excellent places to find barn swallows as they skim the surface, dipping, swerving, swooping and turning to hunt flying insects of all kinds. They will dip their bills into the water for a drink, and bathe on-the-fly as well.

TIP: Make a small mudhole to provide nesting material for swallows. This is especially important if there isn't a lake, stream or wetland fairly close by, or if the weather is dry.

Parks, golf courses, large lawns, pastures and playfields all attract swallows as well, because the open country leaves plenty of room for in-flight insect hunting. Flies and mosquitoes are preferred prey, but moths, butterflies and other insects also end up in barn swallow beaks. Some studies have shown that barn swallows fly over 500 miles per day while hunting for food for their hungry nestlings. If the weather turns cold or insects scarce, barn swallows will head for the ground to pick insects off leaves or grass.

TIP: Identify a barn swallow in flight by its deeply-forked tail. Then just sit back and enjoy the birds' graceful air show.

TIP: Barn swallows build nests of mud. If you don't want them on your buildings for some reason, remove the nests as soon as they are built, before eggs are laid. Cover up areas the swallows like for nesting with *dense* wire mesh.

IDENTIFICATION

Getting a real good look at a barn swallow is hard—they always seem to be in swift flight—but the opportunity is a treat. They are not big at 6 to 7¾ inches in length, and much of that is tail. That tail is deeply forked—a key trait that identifies the barn swallow from the cliff swallow (pages 158–159). As for colors, the barn swallow wears deep steel-blue above, buff with rusty-cinnamon accents below, with a rusty throat and forehead patch (hence the species name *rustica*). Barn swallows seem to chatter and twitter constantly; these sounds are very soft though. The call is a persistent *kvit-kvit-kvit*.

NESTING

As described, most nesting now takes place on manmade structures. Rafters and girders are favorite spots. The nest is a cup of mud, grass and weed stems, lined with feathers and any other soft things the swallow can find. Four or 5 white, brown-spotted eggs hatch after 13–17 days (the female takes care of all incubation duties), and fledging takes 18–23 days more.

TIP: Nail a 2 x 4 board to the side of a building (narrow side against the structure) to provide barn swallows with a nesting spot. Under an eave would be the perfect spot. Note that this perfect spot could also draw swallows away from places you'd rather not have them nest.

Cliff Swallow

Petrochelidon pyrrhonota

Gliding flight and a square tail set this cliff-loving swallow apart.

At first glance, it's easy to lump all the swallows together and call things good. But there are easy ways to distinguish between the various species. For cliff swallows, the key is looking at the tail; it is square-tipped in flight, compared to the barn swallow's deeply-forked tail and the tree swallow's slightly-forked one.

The cliff swallow nested in holes in sheer cliff faces before humans came to the continent, and still does nest in places like this. Unfortunately, introduced house sparrows—invasive and aggressive cavity nesters—will come in and evict entire colonies of cliff swallows. This has been devastating to cliff swallow populations, since the birds may not have enough time or energy left to attempt another brood that year.

Still, man has helped in some ways, by building dams and skyscrapers and freeway interchanges, all offering tall, sheer, cliff-like faces where these graceful and beautiful swallows can build their gourd-shaped nests of mud. Like barn swallows, cliff swallows favor sheltered spots such as overhangs and eaves. In general though, cliff swallows are a little more adventuresome in their choice of nesting spots.

TIP: The cliff swallow builds a gourd-shaped nest of mud, entering through a porthole in the side. The nest is usually attached to a vertical surface.

Cliff swallows love open country where they can put their spectacular flight abilities to work, hunting insects on the wing. The flight is smoother than that of the barn swallow, with gliding and graceful swoops in the shape of an ellipse. Large bodies of water attract cliff swallows, but agricultural land, yards, parks and anywhere else with open sweeps of land (and healthy insect populations) will support barn swallows. They occupy appropriate habitats across North America in summer, and migrate to South America to spend the winter.

IDENTIFICATION

As described above, the cliff swallow shows a square tail in flight, versus the barn swallow's forked tail. At 5 to 6 inches in length, this is a very small swallow. The rump is pale buff, and there is a white patch on the forehead. Upper areas are steely blue, almost black, while the belly and chest are creamy white without the rusty twinges seen on the barn swallow. The throat is a deep chestnut color. Cliff swallows chatter and twitter almost endlessy, and have an alarm call that sounds like *kee!* or *keer!*

NESTING

Cliff swallows tend to nest in loose-knit colonies, originally on cliffs but now on many of the manmade structures mentioned. The cliff swallow builds its nest out of mud, reinforcing the structure with grass and weed stems. The gourd-shaped home is stuck to a vertical face or wall of some sort, and the spot is all the more attractive if it offers overhead protection in the form of an overhang or eave. The female lays 4–5 white eggs which she incubates for 13–15 days. Then the parents really go to work to feed the nestlings a pure insect diet until the youngsters fledge between 17 and 20 days later.

TIP: Look for the square tail, buff-colored rump, chestnut throat or white forehead to see if it's a cliff swallow you're watching.

TIP: Water a spot of bare dirt to create mud that swallows can use to build nests.

Tree Swallow

Tachycineta bicolor

A lovely, blue-green and white swallow that nests in tree cavities.

A tree swallow looks beautiful in its coat of metallic blue-green, contrasting with underparts and chin of pearly white. But this pretty swallow is interesting for many other reasons as well.

For one thing, it nests in tree holes, a big departure from the mud-involved nesting habits of other swallows. Cavities in soft wood and old woodpecker holes work equally well. Tree swallows will utilize nest boxes too.

Although the name tree swallow certainly fits the bird's nesting habits, the description also recognizes the bird's habitat preference—wooded areas along lakes, ponds, rivers, streams, marshes and wetlands. Tree swallows seem even more water-oriented than other swallows, and an ideal nesting spot would be right over the water, as far as a tree swallow is concerned.

TIP: Tree swallows nest in cavities and holes in trees.

The tree swallow is also unique because it is the only major North American swallow species to regularly eat seeds and berries. Bayberries are the absolute favorite, but dogwood berries, bulrush seed, red cedar, Virginia creeper and many other fruits and seeds are also taken. In fact, about a third of the tree swallow's diet consists of these types of foods, mostly when the weather is cooler and insects scarce.

This fruit- and vegetable-eating habit allows the tree swallow to stay farther north than other swallows in winter. Some tree swallows winter along the Gulf Coast—the only swallow to have representatives in the U.S. at that time of year—and some individuals will winter as far north as the Carolinas.

Tree swallows are legendary for the enormous flocks that sometimes gather at migration time, especially in fall.

IDENTIFICATION

A very pretty swallow, from 5 to 6¼ inches long, metallic blue or blue-green above and clear white below. The upperparts could even be described as having a steely sheen. The white extends up through the chin to the cheeks. In flight, the tail is only slightly forked compared to the barn swallow's deeply forked tail and the cliff swallow's square tail. Tree swallows fly distinctively, utilizing gliding circles that end in several flaps of the wing and a climb in elevation before gliding again. A big, wheeling flock is a sight to behold, a vision of elegant motion. The call is a single *chit* or *cheet* note. The song: a happy, twittering series.

NESTING

This swallow prefers to nest in tree cavities or old woodpecker holes, and the closer to water the better. Feathers make up the lining of the nest, and tree swallows are very particular about using feathers—and only feathers—for that job. White feathers are especially favored, and the parents are very brave, swooping and chattering at any creature who dares to intrude into the nesting territory. Tree swallows also willingly use nest boxes. The female lays 4–5 white eggs, and incubates them for 12–13 days. The young fledge 13–14 days after that. The young stay dull brown through their first year, and then start molting into the beauty that is an adult tree swallow.

TIP: Tree swallows will nest in boxes. Optimum opening size: 1½ inches. Bluebird nest trails have benefited tree swallows, as the swallows will utilize some of the boxes the bluebirds don't use.

TIP: Tree swallows are almost invariably found near water. If they can, a pair will even nest in a limb or trunk hanging over the water. They love to line their nests with feathers.

Eastern Phoebe

Sayornis phoebe

Tail-wagging flycatcher of the water's edge.

There seem to be as many descriptions of what a phoebe looks like as there are people who write about birds. And that's not surprising, since the bird's plumage is so nondescript and does seem to take on regional variations. Plus, different light casts different looks. In general, a phoebe is brown-gray or olive green above, dusty white below, with a black bill.

What's never in question is how this bird makes its living: it is a true flycatcher.

TIP: Phoebes like to build their mud-and-grass nests under porches, eaves, ledges ... any protected spot. Since they are such good insect eaters, you might want to invite nesting phoebes by placing a nesting platform (as above) or a 2 x 4 board (page 156) in a strategic spot.

Watch for a phoebe perched on a fence post or wire, or a tree branch. The bird will wag its tail—bobbing it downward, not upward—as it waits for prey to buzz by (a fly, dragonfly, wasp, moth or bee for instance). When the unfortunate target gets in range, the phoebe will flutter out, snatch the meal in mid-flight and return to its perch.

Phoebes love waterways (running water especially) with wooded banks, and prefer to set up summer territory along a river, stream or creek. The reason: These riparian areas offer rich, steady hatches of insects. Another thing phoebes love: cliffs. Cliffs and steep embankments were traditional nesting areas. With man's steady advances upon the land, phoebes have adapted well to buildings, bridges, quarries (it will nest on all of them, in sheltered spots). Phoebes especially love bridges—a perfect combination of water to supply food in the form of insect hatches, and a sheer, cliff-like structure to nest upon.

Most flycatchers are fair-weather visitors and move far south, to Central and South America, for the winter. But some eastern phoebes winter as far north as the bottom tier or two of our southeastern states. Phoebes can do this because when insect populations drop low, which they often do even in the South at this time of year, a phoebe will readily eat berries to sustain itself.

IDENTIFICATION

A phoebe is about 7 inches long (sparrow-sized or a little longer), brown-gray or olive green above (head darker than the rest), dusty white below, with a black bill that appears to have been flattened. There is no light-colored ring around the eye, and no wing bars: good clues when trying to confirm whether you're looking at a phoebe or not. Look for the downward tail-bobbing when perched. Listen for the series of *fee-bee* calls, with the second note alternating between being higher-pitched and lower-pitched than the first.

NESTING

A phoebe pair will build a nest of mud and grass (lined with mosses and hair and anything soft the phoebes can find) in a sheltered niche on a cliff face, building ledge or quarry side, the rocky walls of a ravine or a bridge girder. Both parents work to incubate the 5–6 white eggs, until the young phoebes hatch at 14–17 days. Fledging takes 15–16 days more. The parents will try for a second and even a third brood if insect populations seem to be holding up.

▶ Inset: The black phoebe of the Southwest has a lifestyle very similar to the eastern phoebe. This bird is almost all black, but has a white belly.

TIP: A phoebe will perch on the end of a twig, waiting for prey to buzz by. When the fly, wasp or other target is in range, the phoebe will flutter into the air and grab it. If you're close enough, you can hear the "click" or "snap" of the bird's bill.

Purple Martin

Progne subis

Our largest and most beloved swallow, not really purple but a deep blue-black.

Backyards across rural small-town and suburban America are a testament to the purple martin's popularity: Purple martin houses, in various states of repair or disrepair, are a common sight. Unfortunately, many of these apartment homes, originally erected to attract insect-consuming, colony-nesting martins, are taken over by house sparrows or starlings. In the West, purple martins still nest in traditional sites such as holes in tree limbs or even cactus.

Humans have both helped and hurt purple martin populations, especially in the central and eastern states. The birds have long been accustomed to nesting in manmade structures—often in colonies larger than could ever be possible in the limited amount of natural cavities and cliffs available. But starlings and house sparrows, also brought by man, wreak havoc on martin houses, kicking out the occupants and then taking over year after year.

Native Americans of the Southeast erected martin houses—dried, hollowed-out gourds hung in clusters near their gardens. Who knows what the motive was—to attract martins to consume insects that would bite gardeners or ravage plants? Or just for the sheer joy of attracting these friendly, graceful and beautiful birds? There's probably some truth in both theories.

Because they are larger than other swallows, it's easy to identify martins if there is a mixed group of swallows swirling and swooping over a waterway, fairway or yard. Like other swallows, martins prefer to have some water around, if for nothing else than the steady crops of insects produced there.

If you want martins in your yard, erect some nesting structures (see tips). The effort is well worth it, to be able to sit on the steps on a summer's eve, cool drink in hand, watching the grace of martins in flight and listening to their rich, gurgling song.

TIP: To attract purple martins, set up a purple martin apartment house. The birds love to nest in colonies and if you are lucky, you will attract some of these beautiful swallows. Be patient. It may take a couple of seasons for the birds to come.

IDENTIFICATION

A large swallow at 7¾ to 8½ inches in length, a male purple martin is almost black above, with highlights of the glossiest, deepest blue possible. The bird looks almost purple. Males are dark underneath as well, an excellent way to identify them from other swallows, but females and juveniles are gray or white underneath. Flight is gliding and graceful, with quick flaps of the wings propelling the bird into another swoop. Listen for the guttural, rich *chew-wew* call and the gurgling, liquid song.

NESTING

Purple martins evolved nesting on bluffs and cliffs, and in natural cavities in trees and stumps. In the East they still use these places, but have become attuned to manmade nesting structures. Purple martins like company, and nest in colonies. In the West, birds still occupy more traditional nesting habitats. East or West, the female lays 4–5 white eggs and incubates them for 15–16 days. She and the eggs rest comfortably on a mass of grass and other plant material placed in the cavity. The young take a long time to fledge—28–31 days—and the parents build up hundreds of frequent flyer miles in their quest for insect meals for the babies.

TIP: The purple martin is a great insect eater, swooping and swerving and chasing down its prey in flight—a beautiful sight over a summer evening's backyard.

TIP: Here's how to build a purple martin house from a gourd. Drill a 2-inch hole in the bottom, remove the seeds and dry the gourd. Plug that hole, drill a couple small holes for drainage, and create an entrance hole on the side, 2½ inches in diameter. Paint the gourd white and hang in a cluster with half a dozen (or more) other gourds.

▶ Inset: Female purple martin.

Eastern Kingbird

Tyrannus tyrannus

A bold and aggressive bird of farmland, ranchland and other open country.

The name "kingbird" describes perfectly what this member of the flycatcher family thinks about himself: He is proud, bold and aggressive, the self-declared king of his domain. Kingbirds will pester and harass other songbirds for no apparent reason other than the fun of it. And kingbirds are not afraid to take on hawks, owls and crows as well—especially when the predators are threatening nest and nestlings—even landing on the backs of and pecking the large birds.

So it's no wonder the kingbird is a good hunter too. Usually you'll see him perched on a fence post, wire or branch: a good-sized black, gray and white bird waiting for a fly, bee or other insect to buzz by. The kingbird will hop into the air, fluttering along on his wingtips, then snatch the meal out of the air. Kingbirds will also eat berries in season, hovering and fluttering while plucking fruits from the branches.

It's also not surprising that kingbirds set up territories and do not let other kingbirds nest there. The birds love open country such as farms, ranches, roadsides, and the shores of lakes and rivers—places rich in flying insect life. You can find kingbirds, in summer, most anywhere in North America. But once summer winds down and the insect population dwindles, it's time to migrate southward and the birds will flock up for their travels, and be civil to one another again.

TIP: Kingbirds love to perch on fence posts or barbed wire—perfect spots for waiting for an unsuspecting insect to buzz by.

IDENTIFICATION

A simple but good-looking combination of feathers comprises the Eastern kingbird: dark gray on top (almost black on the head), but white on the chest and belly. The black on the head extends from the beak, back under the eye, to the nape of the neck. A key identifier is the prominent white tip on the tail, very visible in flight. Eastern kingbirds also have a red crown patch (top of the head) but this is usually covered up. A kingbird is about 9 inches long, robin-sized. The call has a sputtering and bickering sound, suitable considering the bird's personality; this sounds like an ascending *killy-killy-killy-killy*. The bird also has other chattering calls in its repertoire.

NESTING

A kingbird will choose a tree or shrub, and build a nest of grass, weed stems and other plant material, lining it with hair, finer pieces of grass and roots. The female lays 3–4 creamy, brown-blotched eggs there, and incubates them by herself for 12–13 days. The male will bring her food during the days before the young hatch. Fledging takes 13–14 more days.

▶ Shown at right: Eastern kingbird.

TIP: Bees are a favorite food, and a wild colony or even a set of hives might attract a pair of kingbirds to set up shop nearby.

Western Kingbird

Tyrannus verticalis

The western kingbird (left) often inhabits the same areas as the Eastern kingbird, especially in the West and Midwest. Where the West gets arid, you'll find kingbirds along the riverbottoms. Identify a western kingbird by its gray head (versus black for the Eastern kingbird) and its yellow belly. There is a band of darker gray through the eyes. The tail is black, with white sides (no white tip). Western kingbirds are so bold as to occasionally nest in the same trees as golden eagles or great horned owls.

Hummingbirds

For such a tiny package, a hummingbird in the garden stirs huge excitement. One of the most rewarding aspects of having hummingbirds visit is knowing that the flowers you planted had a direct effect on getting the birds to come. In the East, if you get a hummingbird, it's a foregone conclusion (except in the rarest of cases) that you are looking at a ruby-throated hummingbird. But a much broader array of hummers calls the West home.

No matter where you live, here's how to get hummingbirds in your garden, identify them, and understand their lifestyle.

Ruby-Throated Hummingbird

Archilochus colubris

Our tiniest bird, this nectar-lover is magnificent looking and fascinating to behold.

*I*t seems odd yet fitting that such a tiny bird (only 3½ inches in length and weighing but 6 to 8 grams) can generate such huge interest. But once you see a couple of ruby-throated hummingbirds, and then become skilled at attracting them to your home, yard and garden, you will feel as though you are their friend and benefactor and protector. Just watching these bundles of energy in action warms the soul and makes you feel good.

Hovering in the air with wings beating so fast they hum, a hummingbird can fly forward and backward with ease (the only bird that can do so), and hover in front of a flower to sip nectar. The wings beat as many as 75 times per second to achieve these aerial feats, and a hummingbird can fly as fast as 60 miles per hour. You have to believe a hummer needs some rest sometime, but the bird rarely sits still—resting only momentarily on a twig or wire before launching off again in fairytale flight.

Of course, all this activity requires a lot of energy, and that's what the high-sugar content of nectar does for a hummingbird. A hummer will feed anywhere from 5 to 10 times per hour, for up to a minute at each session, and will eat up to 30% of its body weight in nectar in a day! Opportunists at heart, hummingbirds will also eat tiny insects, aphids and spiders they find on the flowers from which they sip nectar.

Imagine eating 20% of your body weight in sugar each day. But then think about a hummingbird's metabolism and energy needs: a heart that beats over 1,200 times per minute, lungs that take 250 breaths per minute at rest, and a 500-mile migration step directly over the Gulf of Mexico each spring and fall. Fortunately, a hummingbird can increase its body weight by 50% before either of these flights; and all that fat will burn off in the flight.

At night, a hummingbird at rest conserves energy by dropping its heart rate to 50 beats per minute, slowing its breathing dramatically and dropping its body temperature. If a hummer didn't do these things, it would have to eat all night as well.

(continued)

TIP: Red flowers attract hummingbirds. Since the birds can't smell, they rely on bright colors to find food. Other colors will work too, but red seems to do the best job.

TIP: A hummingbird nest is smaller than a walnut and camouflaged with lichens.

IDENTIFICATION

Once you see a hummingbird in flight, you'll know it: you'll hear the humming and see the bird hovering gracefully in front of a plant, flitting back and forth to different flowers. A male is metallic green above and white below, with a brilliant red throat patch called a *gorget*. A female's throat is white. Refracting light makes the gorgeous hummingbird colors shimmer and shine; if you look at a feather with the light coming from behind, it just looks gray. A long, graceful bill is perfect for sipping nectar from flowers. Hummingbirds do call, but mostly make a chattering squeak, almost mouse-like; and birds make tiny squeals when chasing each other.

NESTING

Males do a graceful, diving display when courting a female. After mating, he hits the road and leaves the female to all nesting and child-rearing duties. The nest is tiny—about the size of half a walnut!—and woven of plant down stuck together with spider silk. Lichens are applied to the outside of a nest, so it is camouflaged superbly. Usually this nest is placed on a branch already covered with lichens and is on the fork of a couple of twigs, often at the end of a branch overhanging a clearing, stream or road's edge. The female lays but 2 white eggs that incubate for about 16 days. Fledging takes about 20–22 days, once the eggs hatch. Of course the female is super-busy feeding the young before they fledge, and they will stay with her until she shoos them off, after fledging. She may then attempt a second brood.

▶ Inset: Male showing black throat.

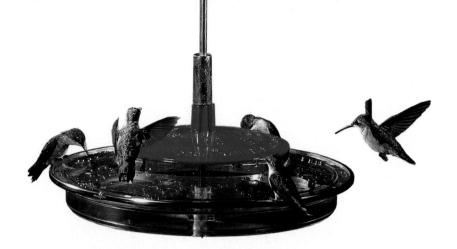

TIP: Many sugar-water feeders are available, and most do a good job of feeding hummingbirds. Make your own sugar-water nectar (see recipe below), and clean the feeder often, as mold can grow there. Hang the feeder near flowers, but at a height and position where you can enjoy watching your visitors; hummingbirds will come very close to your house, deck, patio or window.

Ruby-throated hummingbirds grace the Eastern half of our country during the warm-weather months—namely, when flowers are in bloom. This timing varies with latitude of course, but it makes sense that the birds are not going to be around until there are a lot of flowers from which to sip nectar. Favored habitats vary, but woodlands, meadows, parks and gardens are all attractive.

Ruby-throated hummingbirds travel straight across the Gulf of Mexico to winter in southern Mexico, the Yucatán Peninsula and Central America. There they find the flowers they need to fatten up again for the return flight back to the United States the next spring. It is truly amazing that such a tiny bird can make such a huge flight—across the Gulf of Mexico—and many in fact don't make it. But the strongest survive, ready to return again as one of our most gorgeous and enthralling birds of summer.

SUGAR-WATER NECTAR FOR HUMMINGBIRD FEEDERS

1 part sugar
4 parts water

Mix the sugar and water in a pot. Bring to a boil, and boil for 2 minutes. Cool down the mixture before filling any feeder. Store the rest of the mixture in the refrigerator (an old, cleaned-out juice carton or milk jug works fine). Replace the nectar solution in your feeders at least every three days, to keep it fresh, attractive and safe for hummingbirds.

(Red coloring is not needed; instead use a feeder with plenty of red on it, to attract the hummers.)

▶ Female ruby-throat feeding young.

TIP: While red flowers are most effective at attracting hummingbirds, other colors will work as well, especially orange and yellow. What may be more important than the color is the shape of the flower. Tube-shaped flowers seem to produce more nectar and allow the hummer to be at an advantage, with its long bill, to really dip in and sip the sweet juices.

Gallery of Western Hummingbirds

While the ruby-throated hummingbird inhabits the Eastern half of our country, the West is blessed with its own wonderful and wide variety of hummingbirds.

The principles for attracting hummingbirds in the West are the same as with eastern ruby-throats—flowers, sugar-water feeders and a little water. In fact, all the attracting principles on pages 170–172 apply to western hummers as well; also see the plant lists provided on pages 178–179.

Half the fun of having hummingbirds around your western desert, foothill, mountain, riverbottom, coastal or suburban home is the challenge of identifying your visitors not just as a hummingbird, but as a specific species. This gallery of western hummingbirds will help you in that challenge.

Black-Chinned Hummingbird

Archilochus alexandri

Our most widespread western hummingbird.

Black-chinned hummingbirds are closely related to ruby-throats, but inhabit streamside and other lush areas—always prime real estate in the arid West—from Texas on up through the Rockies and into British Columbia. Black-chins are unique among hummingbirds in that they do not coat the outside of their nests with lichens; it is coated with down, feathers and silk. Offer a little water in a shallow dish—or even very light, fine mist—to give black-chins even more reason to keep coming back to the area of your sugar-water feeder and flower beds.

Both males and females are shimmering green above and white below. The female has a white throat, very finely streaked. The male's throat is black, but appears as an iridescent purple if you get the sun shining on it just right. Black-chinned hummingbirds measure about 3¾ inches in length, about the same as a ruby-throat.

Anna's Hummingbird

Calypte anna

Named for the beautiful wife of a French nobleman and naturalist.

This beautiful hummingbird of the West Coast gives a dramatic and spectacular aerial display. The males climb and then dive from 60 to 120 feet up in the air to impress a potential mate and warn intruders to stay away. The males are also very aggressive about their territory, defending it vigorously from intruders big and small. Anna's hummingbirds sing as well—the only North American hummer to do so—a very prolonged and high-pitched warble. This is a hardy little hummingbird—the only one to winter anywhere in North America; and, Anna's hummingbirds have been known to nest as early as December along the California coast.

The female is predominantly an iridescent green above, creamy or white below, with some red spotting on the throat. Males have iridescent, rose-colored heads, and more green than creamy white below.

Broad-Tailed Hummingbird

Selasphorus platycerus

Hummingbird of the Rocky Mountains.

The broad-tailed hummingbird takes over where the ruby-throat leaves off, and is the hummingbird-in-residence of the Mountain West. Broad-tails never settle too long in one area, keeping on the move as the flowers bloom in the different areas and elevations of their mountain homes. For instance, summer starts early in the valleys and foothills, but as the flowers dry up as summer advances, new blooms appear up in the alpine slopes and meadows, and broad-tails follow the blooms. Look for the birds along clear mountain brooks—in canyon bottoms, where there's some brush and an abundance of moisture for woodland wildflowers; meadows are always close by, as well.

A female is green on the back and top of the head, but white below with some cinnamon accents on the sides. A male looks very similar to a male ruby-throat, with a beautiful rosy-red gorget.

Calliope Hummingbird

Stellula calliope

North America's smallest hummingbird.

A big calliope hummingbird might stretch 3½ inches, but 3 inches is more like it. That's tiny, even in hummingbird terms! This is another hummingbird of the Mountain West. Calliopes will nest far up a mountain—so far that, late at night, the mother will usually keep the last meal of the day for herself and not her tiny chicks, so that she has enough energy to keep them warm until the sun warms their world again. The nest is well insulated, with plenty of downy materials lining it, and placed under an overhanging branch or ledge.

These are absolutely gorgeous hummingbirds, named for the male's iridesent purple streaks on the throat (reminiscent of a calliope). Females have just a bit of rufous coloring on the sides, and instead of the gaudy purple streaks on the throat, have finer gray streaks there.

Rufous Hummingbird

Selasphorus rufus

Aggressive defender of its territory, nests as far north as Alaska.

The rufous hummingbird is known for its aggressive behavior with intruders of all sizes that dare venture into its territory. It is also very unique in how far north it nests—from Montana, Idaho, Oregon and Washington right on up through British Columbia and into coastal Alaska. Rufous hummingbirds will try to raise a couple of broods a season, nesting low to the ground in a coniferous forest in spring and higher up in deciduous trees in summer.

The male is rufous or reddish brown colored on the sides, tail and back, and has a beautiful orange-red gorget that can look almost gold in bright sunlight. The female looks very similar to an Anna's hummingbird female, but the latter has a green back and a green patch on the head.

Costa's Hummingbird

Calypte costae

Hummingbird of the desert.

As with other species, different hummingbirds have adapted to different niches and regions, and here is the desert's representative. Costa's hummingbirds will nest in cactus, sage and even dry yucca plants, building a tiny nest from 1 to 8 feet off the ground. Loose nesting colonies have been found, and this is unique among hummingbirds. These colonies are, quite possibly, the result of an especially good flower crop in the area; the birds tolerate each other's presence in the abundance of good forage. The other limiting factor that could gather birds is water—always a prime commodity in the desert.

    A male Costa's hummingbird has iridescent purple on top of the head as well as on his throat. Like the male, the female has a green back, but she does not have the male's beautiful purple accents.

Allen's Hummingbird

Selasphorus sasin

With a fiery, orange-red throat.

This hummingbird of California migrates northward along the coast, as early as late January and February, sticking to areas where flowers are in bloom. After breeding season is complete, Allen's hummingbirds will move south along the foothills of the Sierras—anywhere from August through September— to take advantage of the blooming flowers inland, thus completing an oval-shaped circuit for the year.

    A male Allen's hummingbird is very beautiful, with rufous sides and back, an orange-red gorget, and a green crown and back. Females are not as rufous overall, trending more toward green, with a white belly and green-streaked gorget.

Hummingbird Plants

Of all the birds you can attract to your yard and garden, hummingbirds are among the most fun to lure in with plants; but you'll need the right ones to do it! The flowers, shrubs, vines and even trees listed here will do a good job attracting hummingbirds—not just ruby-throats, but the spectacular hummingbirds of the West and Southwest as well. Your best bet is to choose and use a variety of plants, for several reasons:

- You have a better chance of finding flowers that will really bring in—and keep—hummers in your garden.
- Different plant species and varieties, with different bloom times, will stretch the flower season in both directions. This will extend your hummingbird season as well. With some planning, you can make this work.
- Some plants may not do well in your area in general, or in the specific micro-climates of your hummingbird garden; if not, all is not lost.

Use plantings including the flowers listed here to really grab the attention of hummingbirds passing through. Then have several varieties of feeders hung nearby, to offer a steady supply of food to hold the birds in your area.

Hummingbird Plants in General

FLOWERING ANNUALS, PERENNIALS AND BULBS:

Bee Balm	*Monarda* spp.	Hollyhock	*Althea* spp.
Begonia	*Begonia* spp.	Impatiens	*Impatiens* spp.
Blazing Star	*Liatris* spp.	Lantana	*Lantana camara*
Bleeding Heart	*Dicentra* spp.	Lily	*Lilium* spp.
Butterfly Weed	*Asclepias tuberosa*	Lupine	*Lupinus* spp.
Canna	*Canna generalis*	Nasturtium	*Tropaeolum* spp.
Cardinal Flower	*Lobelia cardinalis*	Indian Paintbrush	*Castilleja* spp.
Carpet Bugle	*Ajuga reptans*	Penstemon	*Penstemon* spp.
Century Plant	*Agave americana*	Petunia	*Petunia* spp.
Columbine	*Aquilegia* spp.	Phlox	*Phlox* spp.
Coral Bells	*Heuchera sanguinea*	Red-Hot Poker	*Kniphofia uvaria*
Dahlia	*Dahlia* spp.	Scabiosas	*Scabiosa* spp.
Dame's Rocket	*Hesperis matronalis*	Scarlet Sage	*Salvia splendens*
Delphinium	*Delphinium* spp.	Spider Flower	*Cleome spinosa*
Fire Pink	*Silene virginica*	Sweet William	*Dianthus barbatus*
Flowering Tobacco	*Nicotiana alata*	Verbena	*Verbena* spp.
Four o' Clock	*Mirabilis jalapa*	Yucca	*Yucca* spp.
Foxglove	*Digitalis* spp.	Zinnia	*Zinnia* spp.
Fuchsia	*Fuchsia* spp.		
Gilia	*Gilia* spp.		
Geranium	*Pelargonium* spp.		
Gladiolus	*Gladiolus* spp.		

Good Hummingbird Flowers by Region

NORTHEAST/MIDWEST
Wild Columbine *(Aquilegia canandenis)*
Coral Bells *(Heuchera sanguinea)*
Bee Balm *(Monarda didyma)*
Trumpet Honeysuckle *(Lonicera sempervirens)*
Butterfly Bush *(Buddleia davidii)*
Flowering Quince *(Chaenomeless japonica)*

SOUTHEAST
Jewelweed *(Impatiens capensis)*
Standing Cypress *(Ipomopis rubra)*
Bee Balm *(Monarda didyma)*
Cardinal Flower *(Lobelia cardinalis)*
Scarlet Sage *(Salvia coccinea)*
Trumpet Creeper *(Campsis radicans)*
Red Buckeye *(Aesculus pavia)*

WESTERN MOUNTAINS
Indian Paintbrush *(Castilleja* spp.*)*
Fireweed *(Epilobium angustifolium)*
Scarlet Gilia *(Ipomopsis aggregata)*
Horsemint *(Monarda fistulosa)*
Orange Honeysuckle *(Lonicera ciliosa)*
Flowering Currant *(Ribes gordonianum)*

SOUTHWEST
Bouvardia *(Bouvardia ternifolia)*
Parry's Penstemon *(Penstemon parryi)*
Autumn Sage *(Salvia greggii)*
Lemmon's Sage *(Salvia lemmonii)*
Red Morning Glory *(Ipomoea coccinea)*
Chuparosa *(Justica californica)*
Red Bird-of-Paradise *(Caesalpinia pulcherrima)*

PACIFIC COAST
Crimson Columbine *(Aquilegia formosa)*
Indian Paintbrush *(Castilleja californica)*
Fuchsia *(Fuchsia* hybrids*)*
Red-Hot Poker *(Kniphofia uvaria)*
Scarlet Monkeyflower *(Mimulus cardinalis)*
Red-Flowering Currant *(Ribes sanguineum)*
Fuchsia-Flowering Gooseberry *(Ribes speciosum)*

SHRUBS:

Abelia	*Abelia grandiflora*
Azalea	*Rhododendron* spp.
Bearberry	*Arctostaphylos* spp.
Beauty Bush	*Kokwitzia amabilis*
Beloperone	*Beloperone californica*
Butterfly Bush	*Buddleia davidii*
Cape Honeysuckle	*Tecomaria capensis*
Currant	*Ribes odoratum*
Flowering Quince	*Chaenomeless japonica*
Gooseberry	*Ribes speciosum*
Hardy Fuchsia	*Fuchsia magellanica*
Hibiscus	*Hibiscus* spp.
Honeysuckle	*Lonicera* spp.
Jasmine	*Jasminum* spp.
Weigela	*Weigela* spp.

VINES:

Cypress Vine	*Quamoclit* spp.
Honeysuckle	*Lonicera heckrottii*
Morning Glory	*Ipomoea* spp.
Scarlet Runner-Bean	*Phaseolus coccineus*
Trumpet Creeper	*Campsis radicans*
Trumpet Honeysuckle	*Lonicera sempervirens*

TREES:

Chaste Tree	*Vitex agnus-castus*
Chinaberry	*Melia azedarach*
Cockspur Coralbean	*Erythrina cristi-galli*
Eucalyptus	*Eucalyptus* spp.
Flowering Crabapple	*Malus* spp.
Hawthorn	*Crataegus* spp.
Horse Chestnut	*Aesculus hippocastanum*
Locust	*Robinia* spp.
Orange	*Citrus* spp.
Palo Verde	*Parkinsonia floride*
Poinciana	*Caesalpinia* spp.
Red Buckeye	*Aesculus carnea*
Royal Poinciana	*Delonix regia*
Siberian Pea Tree	*Caragana arborescens*
Silk Oak	*Grevillea robusta*
Silk Tree	*Albizia julibrissin*
Tree Tobacco	*Nicotiana glauca*
Tulip Tree	*Liriodendron tulipifera*

Gamebirds & Waterfowl

While many of these birds require very specialized habitats to survive, it's also true that some of them—pheasants, doves, many ducks, geese, even turkeys—will become regular visitors to yard and garden if you're "on the edge" of some wilder areas, even in the suburbs, and you create the right habitat niches. Some of these birds may never come to your yard and garden, but here's a chance to learn more about them and their lifestyle for the time when you do have an opportunity to see them in the wild.

You don't have to hunt to appreciate gamebirds and waterfowl. They're just birds—and quite spectacular and interesting ones at that.

Mourning Dove

Zenaidura macroura

Our most common dove, known for its haunting, mournful song.

Songbird or gamebird? The mourning dove is both, and popular on both fronts. How could anyone shoot a bird so beautiful? Tradition runs strong, and 75% of first-year doves die whether they are hunted or not; the harvest merely makes use of the resource. The birds are highly valued for their superb-tasting meat.

Yet there are always plenty of mourning doves to go around, it seems, because mourning doves are good at making more mourning doves, and these attractive birds are found in every state.

One reason mourning doves do so well, even considering the hunting pressure they take, is because man's activities of clearing land and planting crops have benefited the dove's open-country, seed-eating lifestyle. They have adapted well and thrive with but a few trees around, unlike their very close relative the passenger pigeon which did not fare so well with land use changes.

In addition, a pair of mourning doves will raise up to 5 broods a year, either by themselves or in conjunction with other partners.

Mourning doves are good feeder birds, fairly easily attracted to towns, suburbs and country dwellings. They usually feed on the ground, gleaning seeds such as sunflower, millet, wheat and most any other waste grain, ragweed, weed seed of all descriptions, sorghum, foxtail and many others. Mourning doves like to flock up, especially as the weather turns cold, and you will frequently see these groups picking up grit along roadways. They are fast flyers, and will often travel miles between feeding, watering and roosting spots.

TIP: Mourning doves love to feed on the ground; providing a mown, clear area (that is fairly close to trees or escape cover) is important for attracting the birds.

TIP: Spilled feed from all your other feeders will attract mourning doves. They will visit tray and even some hanging feeders too, if they can fit their long bodies and tails on. The best attracting technique is to spread sunflower, millet or other grain on the ground.

IDENTIFICATION

A mourning dove is about 12 inches long, predominantly brown-buff colored, with black-spotted wings that are pink on the undersides, a black spot on the neck, and powder-blue and rosy twinges around the neck area. From a distance they're rather plain looking, but elegantly detailed if you're fortunate enough to see one up close. The tail is long for a bird of this size, pointed, usually marked with some white. Females look similar to males, only not quite as bright. Mourning doves are well known for their sad-sounding song, a low *hoo-ah hoo, hooo, hooo*; the last two *hoo's* are very soft.

NESTING

Mourning doves go through a rather elaborate courtship ritual, with the male bowing to the female and following her about. The two preen each other and even "kiss" by touching beaks. The nest is a flimsy, almost laughable affair of twigs and sticks in a bush or tree, often an evergreen; sometimes you can see the eggs through the nest's bottom. The male incubates by day, the female by night. The two white eggs hatch in 14–15 days, and the young fledge in 14 more. Both parents work to raise the young, feeding them "pigeon's milk," a nutritious mix produced in the parents' crops from seeds eaten and then regurgitated into the babies' waiting mouths.

Bobwhite Quail

Colinus virginianus

Handsome little quail of grasslands and farmlands, named for its bob-white *call.*

Bobwhites are lovely little quail of the central and eastern United States, offering many endearing traits.

First of all, they are homebodies—usually living in a home range of 40 acres or less. A bobwhite will live its entire life on this little area. Bobwhites live in coveys of 10 to 25 birds, and when a covey flushes at your feet they go whirring off in every direction of the compass. Then listen for their distinctive *hoo-ha-hoo* call as they try to regroup.

TIP: Bobwhites roost in a circle, tails in and heads out, to get all eyes looking outward and watching for predators. The strategy also conserves energy on cold nights.

When roosting at night, bobwhites will form a ring, with their tails together and every member of the covey facing outward; this helps them watch for predators, and conserves energy while keeping the birds warm. The only time of year bobwhites really leave the security of their covey is during the nesting season, when pairs break off to raise their broods.

The bobwhite's diet consists of weed and grass seeds, supplemented by insects in the summer, when parents are raising young. Berries are relished when they are accessible, as are acorns and pine seeds.

Bobwhites have both benefited and suffered with man's use of the land. There are certainly more bobwhites now than when unbroken forests covered the East; the farmland—with all its grains, grasslands, pastures, brushy fencelines and forested edges—once provided almost ideal conditions for bobwhites. In some areas, almost every farm had a "home" covey or two. But with advancements in agriculture—such as bigger tractors that need big fields and not lots of brush and fencerows—bobwhite populations have declined as the small family farm goes by the wayside and land is cleared and cleaned in the name of progress.

Hunting literature is filled with lore of, and reverence for, the bobwhite—a gentleman's gamebird. But it is the use of the land that has always dictated the bobwhite's fate. They are lovely birds, a true symbol of America's heartland.

IDENTIFICATION

A small and chunky bird, only 8 to 11 inches long and weighing between 6 and 8 ounces. The back is brown mottled with gray and black; the undersides are lighter —buffy white and delicately streaked. A cock (shown large at right) has a white throat and eyebrow, while the female's face is patterned with buff in those places. Listen for the male's *bob-white* call. Both males and females give a *hoo-ha-hoo* call when a covey has been flushed and the individuals are trying to regroup.

NESTING

The male bobwhite courts females with his namesake song, then the pair scratches out a depression on the ground, lining it with grass and covering part of it with a dome of grass and weed stalks. Both parents work together to incubate the 10–15 creamy white eggs, which hatch in 22–23 days. The young fledge only 6–7 days after that, then follow their parents out into the world to grab high-protein insects, and ultimately learn about eating seeds and berries.

TIP: Bobwhites love grassy areas that are interspersed with brush and even woodlots. These quail will live happily quite close to man and buildings, if the habitat is right.

▶ Inset: Female bobwhite.

TIP: Spread grain—cracked corn or oats or sorghum all work well—to attract feeding bobwhites.

California Quail

Callipepla californica

Plumed quail of the Far West.

This striking bird—resplendent in its plumage of russet, blue-gray and white topped off with a distinctive plume—resides in foothills and mountain valleys west of the continental divide from British Columbia through Washington and Oregon, through California and into Baja Mexico. 4,000 feet seems the upper limit of elevation these quail will readily inhabit. They like mountain valleys and foothills, with plenty of grasslands, savannahs and other openings. Chapparal, scrub and even suburban areas all hold birds.

Water is a key component, and probably the limiting factor, of California quail habitat. The birds live in the very arid regions within their range, and need standing water daily (see tip). In fact, California quail populations seem to ebb and flow with rainfall. In years where adequate moisture falls, the birds do well; if it's dry, populations decline. In the long run, things even out.

Of course, the birds need water to drink. But rainfall also helps grow the food they like to eat—seeds, berries, and the leaves of forbs and grasses. When they can get it, California quail also relish wheat and other small grains, as well as clover and alfalfa seeds. California quail stick close to brushy cover, venturing into open areas to feed at dawn and dusk.

Like bobwhites, California quail are covey birds, preferring to live in close-knit groups of 10 or 20, but sometimes up to 50, birds. Breeding season finds coveys dispersing for nesting duties, but the covey joins back together, successfully reared young in tow, by midsummer. In winter, coveys will converge to form huge flocks of up to 500 birds that will stick to the thickest and best cover in a township or river valley.

TIP: California quail feed on the ground. Scatter cracked corn, wheat or other small grains to attract them to your yard or garden at feeding time.

TIP: California quail like brushy cover interspersed with grassy openings and areas. If there are some wild places around—they don't have to be fancy—whether on land you might own or elsewhere, work to keep them open and undeveloped.

IDENTIFICATION

Male and female California quail are absolutely stunning birds, with "scaled" blue-gray and white chests and russet flanks. It's hard to describe the full interaction of the lovely yet muted colors! The tear-drop shaped plume is prominent, and it is larger on the male than on the female. The other way to tell a male from a female: The male has a black chin and cap, both outlined in white, compared to the female's grayish face. Listen for the call—*chi-CA-go*—the birds use to locate each other and gather up the covey after they are flushed.

NESTING

Males will give a crowing song from fence posts or wires, or atop a bush, to attract a female. The nest is just a grass-lined, hollowed-out depression on the ground. It is usually built in tall weeds, or beside a log or boulder. The hen lays 12–16 cream-colored, brown-speckled eggs. She will incubate the eggs for 21–23 days, but the male stays close by and will take over if she is killed. Both parents care for the brood after the eggs hatch, and the young fledge in about 10 days.

TIP: Offer water—either in a small man-made pond or even a birdbath, to attract California quail. If you get a covey coming, keep replenishing the water supply, as they will depend on it.

Gallery of Quail

In addition to the bobwhite and California quail, four other quail species inhabit the United States. They all reside in various niches across the West.

Scaled Quail

Callipepla squamata

A true—and blue—desert quail.

Here is the quail of the deserts and arid grasslands of the Southwest. A scaled quail is bluish gray with feathers edged in black, giving the bird a scaled appearance. Males and females look very similar, but the male's crest is a little longer and whiter. Like other quails, scaled quail (also, fittingly enough, called blue quail) live most of the year in coveys, dispersing only for nesting season. A bird might be born, live and die on one 80-acre tract.

Water makes or breaks the scaled quail's year. If adequate rainfall comes, nesting is completed and some young will survive the long, hot and dry summer. If it is a dry year, scaled quail may not even attempt to nest, conserving the energy instead for when the effort can actually be successful.

Mearn's Quail

Cyrtonyx montezumae

Another desert quail, also known as Harlequin Quail.

These fascinating-looking little quail are true homebodies, and often live their lives on only 10 acres. The male's impossibly complex but stunning plumage consists of an intricate black-and-white mask on the face, a rust-colored crest, a chest of cinnamon or black, and wings and flanks heavily spotted with white. Hens are overall buff and cinnamon colored, without the male's facial markings or bold flecks of white.

Texas, New Mexico and Arizona all have some Mearn's quail. And, as the Latin name *montezumae* suggests, the birds also inhabit a good portion of Mexico's arid western areas.

Mountain Quail

Oreortyx pictus

Our largest quail, inhabitant of rugged, high-altitude country.

The mountains of Idaho, Oregon, Washington, Nevada and California are blessed with the handsome, plumed mountain quail. Mountain quail spend summer and fall in small family coveys of 10 or so birds, at altitudes of up to 10,000 feet in elevation. They like brushlands mixed with conifers. For winter, the birds may move as much as 15 or 20 miles to find milder weather conditions and better cover in a protected valley or canyon at much lower elevation.

The plume is long and straight on a mountain quail. The chest, neck and head are blue-gray, and there is a chestnut-colored patch, trimmed with white, on the throat. The lower underparts are chestnut-colored with white bars. Cocks and hens look similar, but the hens are a little duller. Fruits and berries make up the bulk of the mountain quail's diet—snowberry, serviceberry, wild grapes and hackberry are staples. Acorns, grass seeds, tubers and some insects are also eaten.

Gambel's Quail

Callipepla gambelii

Desert quail of the extreme Southwest.

The Gambel's quail inhabits some of the toughest country the Southwest can dish out. Many biologists believe that Gambel's quail can survive without standing water, getting by on just the moisture they get from succulent plants. That trait puts Gambel's quail in different country than the other desert quails—scaled and Mearn's—which need standing water to survive. The best place to find Gambel's quail is along the base of a range of desert hills or mountains, where any moisture that does fall will flow, providing some moisture for succulent plant growth.

With their teardrop-shaped plume, a male Gambel's quail resembles a cock California quail. But a Gambel's belly doesn't have a scale-like appearance; the bird is overall more of a bluish gray color, and he has a black belly patch. Plus, a male Gambel's has a russet-colored cap. A female Gambel's quail lacks the black facemask and belly patch, but still has a plume.

Ring-Necked Pheasant

Phasianus colchicus

Brilliantly-colored import from the Orient.

Although several imported birds—such as the starling and house sparrow—have taken hold successfully in North America, none have been as welcome as the ring-necked pheasant. Imported from China to Oregon in the 1880s, pheasants took a quick liking to grassland-grainfield-wetland-farmland habitat, quickly spread and were stocked in many more places, and soon became one of America's favorite game birds.

Although pheasants are occasionally blamed for ousting native prairie chickens and sharp-tailed grouse, the bigger culprit was the plow (and the cow) that destroyed the wild and native prairie. Pheasants—long adapted to agricultural areas and willing to live in small home ranges—filled the void. As farming practices changed to larger farms and much grassy and brushy cover was destroyed in the 1960s and 1970s, pheasants suffered huge losses, but they have been doing better since the Conservation Reserve Program restored grasslands and cover in agricultural areas, beginning in the 1980s.

Pheasants also do well near humans—in the country, on the edges of small towns, and in suburban areas with some out-of-the-way weedy corners, small woods and wetlands. Even some urban areas hold pheasants today. Ringnecks will come to seed offerings, and readily nest around the yard and garden as well, if there's enough cover. They love grass the most, but retreat to cattails, bulrushes, other wetlands and brush during winter. Harsh winters can devastate pheasant populations because snow makes their forage inaccessible.

Adult pheasants eat small grains (corn, wheat, oats, milo, etc.), seeds of all kinds, buds, leaves and insects. The young concentrate on insects early in life—a high-protein diet that helps them grow quickly—before turning to a more adult diet in late summer and autumn. Wild fruits and berries are also eaten. In winter, pheasants will congregate in larger flocks of a dozen to a hundred birds, to take advantage of cover and available food sources; they will disperse across the countryside in spring to go about their breeding duties.

TIP: Pheasants love grassland cover with plenty of brushy and other edges. They don't ask for much, and will live in towns and suburbs.

IDENTIFICATION

Few birds can match a male ring-necked pheasant for stunning beauty. He sports an iridescent purple-green head, bold red eye patch, stunning white ring around the neck, copper-red-brown body feathers and powder-blue rump patch. The tail feathers are incredible and can take up 2 feet of the rooster's 30 to 36-inch total length. A rooster may weigh between 2½ and 3 pounds. A female looks vastly different—a mottled sandy brown, cream and gray—but she is beautiful as well in her own subdued, elegant way. Her total length is 21 to 25 inches, the tail is shorter than the male's, and weight is 1½ to 2¼ pounds. Listen for the male's loud, raspy *kyik-kuk* crow during the spring and early summer breeding season as he tries to attract a mate to his territory. He makes a loud, raspy *kick-kick, kick-kick, kick-kick* cackle when flushed.

NESTING

Roosters (males) crow loudly in spring, trying to lure a female to mate and then nest in his territory. The hen will scrape a depression in a grassy area, line it with grass stalks and feathers, then lay 6–15 olive-brown eggs. She completes all incubation and chick-raising duties; the male is too brightly colored and would attract predators. The eggs hatch in 23–24 days, and the young fledge only 6–7 days after that, heading out into the world to hunt insects with their mother. Delayed mowing in roadside ditches and hayfields would save many, many pheasant nests each year.

TIP: Scatter shelled corn to attract pheasants. In winter, build a simple lean-to feeder with plywood and 2 x 4's to keep snow off the grain so that pheasants can reach it.

▶ Inset: Hen pheasant.

Ruffed Grouse

Bonasa umbellus

Thunder and drumming in the woodlands.

*I*f you're ever on a woodland walk and a roar of wingbeats startles you as a reddish brown or gray bird streaks away through the tree branches, you've flushed a ruffed grouse. And, if you're fortunate enough to be in or near the forest in early spring, for whatever reason, you may hear what sounds like a tractor starting in the distance; a slow thumping at first, gradually speeding up and then ending in a flurry of beats. That also is a ruffed grouse—this time, a male "drumming" atop a log to attract a female for mating.

TIP: Good grouse habitat is thick with small trees and shrubs, but the forest floor is not grassy. Young aspens are prime areas to find grouse, but so is any other area that has been logged within the last decade to fifteen years.

Although they are quite vocal in these ways, ruffed grouse are really shy and secretive birds, preferring to reside in dense brush and woodlands; aspens are a favorite habitat, as are oak forests. But within their range, any thick, brushy cover that offers plenty of fruits, buds and catkins (preferred foods from shrubs and trees) could harbor a few ruffs. Old apple orchards are wonderful spots to find ruffed grouse.

Although they haven't taken to civilization as well as the popular and imported ring-necked pheasant, ruffed grouse will live close to human habitation and can become quite tame. As for overall populations, ruffed grouse have probably benefited from man's changes to and logging of the land—activities that keep forests young and thick (second and third growth), the kind of habitat ruffed grouse like.

Grouse are homebodies, spending their entire life in maybe 40 acres. Winter may be one of the ruffed grouse's easiest times of year, if there's enough snow available, because they have a habit of diving into the snow to roost at night. These snow roosts are warmer than being exposed to the night air, and they also offer safety from predators. In winter, abundant tree buds, well above the snow, feed the birds.

Ruffs aren't covey birds, but you will see groups congregated around food sources such as ripe dogwood or other berries; family groups also stay together until early to mid autumn, when dispersal takes place and the young head out—often walking many miles—to find a home territory of their own.

Ruffed grouse are popular gamebirds across their range; they are usually so wily and wild that there is little chance hunting can really hurt population levels. Winter weather, nesting season weather, food supply, other predators and the grouse's 10-year population cycle all have a larger effect on population levels.

TIP: If you're fortunate to live near grouse, here are some ways to attract them. Leave brushy areas intact; plant dogwood because ruffs relish the ripening berries, as well as the ones that fall to the ground; let "weed" trees like aspen grow; if you have walking paths in or near woods, plant them with clover.

IDENTIFICATION

Ruffed grouse display a long, beautiful and rounded "fan" of tail feathers that is bordered by a dark band near the tip. There is a luxurious black or chestnut-colored "ruff," usually with flavors of iridescent green, around the neck. Many color phases exist, but red and gray are predominant and the others are some combination thereof. The farther north you go, the more gray birds you seem to see; the farther south, the more red-phase birds. Ruffed grouse are good-sized—about 15 to 20 total inches long, and weighing 1 to 1½ pounds. They are not very vocal, except for the flurry of wingbeats upon a flush, and the male's drumming. They will cluck and peep, sort of like a chicken, when alarmed.

NESTING

The male drums—atop an old log, boulder or other vantage point—to attract a female to mate and nest in his territory. The hen will make a shallow depression at the base of a tree or shrub—always in a place with heavy overhead cover—and lay 8–14 buff-colored eggs. The chicks will hatch in about 24 days, and be up and walking within a day or two after that. Good weather is critical at this point—cold and rain can kill the small, downy chicks. The chicks remain with the hen throughout the summer and into the autumn, before dispersing. It is interesting that one hen's brood can have chicks of any and all color phases. The young grouse gradually shift from high-protein insects to the fruits-buds diet that will sustain them the rest of their life.

▶ Inset: Gray-phase male, strutting.

Wild Turkey

Meleagris gallopavo

Largest of the game birds, back from the brink and once again a common sight across its range.

KEY
Wild Turkey
Ranges

- Eastern
- Merriam's
- Gould's
- Florida (Osceola)
- Rio Grande

There was a time, only a few decades ago, when wild turkeys were rare to nonexistent across much of the range they currently call home. Fortunately, for bird lovers of all kinds, all that has changed with stocking and habitat improvement. Eastern wild turkeys love large, forested areas that are broken up with fields, meadows and openings. Their downfall arose from the wholesale cutting of forests, effectively eliminating much of their hiding cover. Then, as some of the land began to revert back to forest, turkeys made a comeback, aided by man's restoration efforts and the bird's great adaptability.

Turkeys are opportunistic feeders, eating everything from grasshoppers and other insects to fruits, grains, acorns and other nuts, even lizards, small toads, frogs and tiny snakes! A bird this big—toms (males) weigh 16 to 28 pounds and hens 8 to 12 pounds—can't afford to pass up any potential meal. Turkeys will group up in the wintertime around good cover and food—often harvested cropfields if available—but spend the rest of the year segregated into smaller groups of hens, jakes (young males) and mature toms. When a group feeds, it usually posts one member as a "lookout" while the others hunt insects and peck for nuts, seeds and fruits.

Five subspecies of this majestic bird reside in various habitats across the U.S., with some birds living in Canada and Mexico as well. The five are: the Eastern, Merriam's, Rio Grande, Florida (also known as Osceola) and Gould's. The accompanying map outlines their ranges.

Of course, the bird has always been an important food source from the time Native Americans hunted it, and it still is hunted, in more and more places each year. But you don't have to hunt them to appreciate wild turkeys; they are magnificent birds in their own right, true symbols of America.

TIP: Wild turkey stocking has brought the bird back from limited distribution. It is a real conservation success story.

TIP: Wild turkeys will live surprisingly close to humans. Spread ear corn to attract wild turkeys if, of course, you're fortunate enough to have a few in your area. You can shell it and offer whole kernels if you wish, but don't worry too much; the birds can do the picking of the kernels. In winter, build an elevated feeder to get the feed off the ground and accessible. Use wire mesh as the tray, to allow drainage if snowmelt occurs.

IDENTIFICATION

Although each subspecies varies somewhat in its look, a few generalizations can be made. Fortunately, there's little doubt as to what you're looking at if you see a turkey standing in the open or foraging through the woods—these birds are *big*. A tom is 36 to 45 inches tall, a hen 26 to 34. The tom is brown/black for the most part, with iridescent sheens of green, blue and purple. The wings are barred, and his head is not feathered, usually bluish, but shows a lot of red during the spring breeding season. A female is smaller and browner: better camouflaged for raising young turkeys to adulthood. Wild turkeys communicate wonderfully with each other, and sometimes it's almost comical to hear them putting, yelping and making *kee-kees* as a group works through the woods or tries to find each other. Toms gobble in spring (see below).

BREEDING

Toms gobble mightily (above) during the spring mating season—huffing, puffing, strutting and fanning their tail to show off and attract a hen. The biggest and baddest tom usually does most of the breeding, and a serviced hen will go off by herself to make a nest under a log or bush and lay 8–14 brown, speckled eggs. She does all incubating duties for 27–28 days, and after 10 days the hatchlings or *poults* are pretty good at evading predators, and can even fly a little bit. They stay with the mother until fall, when the young males break off into their own little cast-off groups.

▶ Inset: Hen turkey (eastern subspecies).

Gallery of Gamebirds

Although you may never have any of these birds residing in your garden, you might at some point be in their domain and want to know what you're seeing.

Chukar Partridge

Alectoris chukar

Imported from the Himalayas, this handsome bird lives in steep, rugged mountainous areas. A mostly gray bird with barred flanks, red legs and a red beak. Listen for the *chukar-chukar-chukar* call.

Sharp-Tailed Grouse

Tympanuchus phasianellus

The prairie grouse, lover of wide-open grasslands as well as mixed brushlands. This bird is subdued looking but still beautiful in its speckled, sandy plumage. The tail is short and pointed—the similar hen pheasant's is much longer. Listen for the *tuk-tuk-tuk* call. Sharptail males dance (see photo) on *leks*—group breeding grounds—in spring.

Prairie Chicken

Tympanuchus spp.

Greater and lesser prairie chickens teemed on the native prairie before cows, crops and fences broke the ecosystem. Protected remnant populations still remain of this brown-gray-and-white, barred bird. The male prairie chicken gives a spectacular courting display, dancing and strutting and showing off yellow air sacs on his neck.

Sage Grouse

Centrocercus urophasianus

The "bomber" of sage country, a mature sage grouse cock might weigh 6 to 7 pounds, with a wingspan of 30 inches. As the name suggests, these birds need sage brush to live, for they eat in it, nest in it, hide in it and breed in it. Sage grouse are mottled gray-brown, with a black belly. Shown: A cock displaying during breeding season.

Blue Grouse

Dendragapus obscurus

The forest grouse of the high mountains, this bird exhibits the quirky behavior of heading *higher* in elevation as winter approaches. Actually the reason is simple: there are more conifers for winter food (needles, buds seeds and twigs) up high. Snow doesn't matter; the grouse will live in the tree branches. Blue grouse are so dusky and deep gray in color, they almost appear blue.

Spruce Grouse

Dendragapus canadensis

Also known as the fool hen, this grouse of the alpine and boreal wilderness loves conifer forests, but also ventures into aspens, birches and boglands. These birds are very dark, brownish gray to black on top, with a black throat and tail (males). Females are lighter-colored overall. Look for the male's red eyecomb.

Hungarian Partridge

Perdix perdix

Also known as "hun," this import from the plains of central Europe has done well in the intensively farmed regions of America's heartland. The bird has filled the niches the prairie grouse (sharptails and prairie chickens) had to abandon when the plow came. Huns are tough birds, surviving winter well even where cover is lacking and icy arctic blasts roll in from the North. They are handsome as well, in their coats of gray and brown.

Mallard

Anas platyrhynchos

Adaptable and widespread, this common duck lives everywhere from wilderness prairie potholes to city parks and yards.

*I*t's easy to forget about how wonderful mallards really are, as common as they have become in many areas. Country and city cousins alike are handsome birds—especially the drake, with his green head, purple wing patch (called the speculum), rusty-chestnut breast and silvery belly.

A mallard is a dabbler, which means: When the duck is in the water feeding, it tips up, tail in the air, as the head bobs underwater to feed on a variety of aquatic plants. Mallards are very fond of grain, too, and will readily eat corn, soybeans, wheat, oats, rice and other grains.

Mallards have adapted well to civilization, as evidenced by the numbers of birds you can see in city and suburban parks and yards. This is in the face of major drainage of wetlands on the North American prairies—the mother lode of wild mallards for the world.

Mallards have the most extensive breeding range of any North American duck, and can be found nesting anywhere within the continental United States, as well as Canada and Alaska. These prolific ducks will also breed with other duck species—including pintails and the closely related black duck, as well as domestic ducks. In fact, most of today's domestic ducks are descended from mallards in some way.

TIP: A mallard "dabbles" for aquatic plants, tipping so that the tail points straight upward as the bird forages just under the surface for aquatic plants.

TIP: If you live on water—pond, lake, river, creek or just a wetland—a nesting platform or basket might attract mallards to raise a brood near you. Even if you're a few blocks to a half mile from water, a hen might nest in your yard or garden if there's a wild, brushy or grassy corner to act as cover.

TIP: Spread corn or sunflower on the ground to attract mallards to a feeding station.

▶ Inset: Hen mallard.

IDENTIFICATION

The drake is distinctive with his iridescent green head (sometimes it has a purple sheen), olive-yellow bill, white neck band, rusty-chestnut breast and silvery-white belly. The female is overall mottled brown, perfect camouflage for her nesting duties. Both males and females feature a purple speculum or wing patch. What can be said about the call, other than: quack! Actually, mallards are highly vocal and their communication is quite fascinating—chuckles, loud warning quacks, clucks and chuckles of contentment, warning quacks for the young … a whole duck language.

NESTING

Breeding season can be a hectic time, with three or more drakes chasing after one hen for breeding rights. But then all the work goes to the hen. She makes a nest of leaves, grass and weed stalks—lining it with down for warmth and softness—hiding it in bulrushes, tall grass or in a brushpile. The hen does all the incubation, and that takes 26–30 days; she covers the eggs with leaves and grass whenever she leaves to feed. The tiny, yellow ducklings are ready to leave the nest only a day after hatching, and this is when you often see a mother leading her line-up of youngsters to the nearest water. It is interesting that you don't have to be right on (or even a stone's throw from) water to have mallards nest in your yard and garden. But the farther the trip to water—and the mother will head for water once hatching is done—the more help the brood might need in getting there; you might want to act as traffic cop.

Wood Duck

Aix sponsa

Our most exquisite and endearing duck—it loves forests with or near water, and nests in tree cavities and nest boxes.

Even the most talented artist, with hundreds of brushes and a complete palette of colors at his or her disposal, could not possibly match what nature's strokes have created with the wood duck. Elegant and ornate, a drake wood duck in breeding plumage will take your breath away. The female does not wear such gaudy plumage, being the one who takes care of all the nesting and duckling-rearing duties, but she is pretty in her own grays and browns.

Wood ducklings emerging from nest hole.

Wood ducks are tree cavity nesters, and at one point in this century their survival was endangered. The culprits: drainage of wetlands and the felling of bottomland forests (which took away nesting habitat). Conservationists realized that hunting seasons needed to close as well, and they did for 23 years. The saviors: tens of thousands of nest boxes, placed by hunters and non-hunters alike, to provide wood ducks with the nesting sites they needed; and some stemming of the rampant wetland draining.

Today, wood ducks are doing well, and it is not an uncommon sight to see one of these stunning birds paddling along a wooded waterway. They like wooded swamps, and marshes, creeks and ponds that are surrounded by forest or at least have some trees around. If you see a couple of crested ducks rise off the water, their high-pitched squeals piercing the air, you've flushed some wood ducks.

Woodies relish acorns as food. If there are not acorns around, they will eat other nuts and seeds. Wood ducks will dabble for aquatic plants as well. Corn and rye are favorite grains.

Wood ducks are not the hardiest of ducks, and they will wait until the leaves are out and the danger of a heavy freeze is past, before making their appearance in spring. They nest both in the Eastern and Western United States, rarely on the Great Plains and only then along some wooded riverbottom. Come fall, wood ducks will head south when the first frosts hit.

TIP: A nest box is a great way to help woodies. Add wood chips to make it seem like a natural cavity, and you might even put a mesh grate inside, to help the young wood ducks climb out.

IDENTIFICATION

A male wood duck displays a rainbow of iridescent greens, purples and blues. The head may be most stunning of all, with a white chin patch, red bill and red eye, and a long sweeping crest of green trimmed with white. At only 17 to 20 inches in length, the woody is a small duck but it is unquestionably our most beautiful. A female is gray-brown, with blue, iridesent wing feathers. Tell her apart from other hen ducks by the crest (not as large as the male's), white throat patch and white oval around the eyes. Wood ducks don't really quack; rather, they whistle a plaintive *hoo-eek hoo-eek* or *creek-creek* cry when flying. On the water, wood ducks will communicate with short, rising *peet* and *cheep* notes.

NESTING

Wood ducks nest in cavities. Of course, the birds evolved using tree cavities, but nowadays wood ducks often nest in manmade nest boxes. In fact, considering man's skill at clearing and draining bottomland forest, the only reasons we have wood ducks today are the nest boxes that helped restore struggling wood duck populations. No matter what the cavity (and it might be 50 feet above the ground if it's an old woodpecker hole) the female fills it with down, then incubates a clutch of 9–15 creamy white eggs for 30 days. Soon thereafter, the young jump from the nesting cavity to the ground, where they bounce once or twice, get up, and follow their mother to water. It is a sight to behold, and makes the work of a nest box worth it.

▶ Inset: Hen wood duck.

Canada Goose

Branta canadensis

The haunting, lonely honking of Canada geese has traditionally been a harbinger of a new season, the V-shaped flock pulling in spring (or winter) behind it as it heads north (or south).

Canada Geese are traditionally a symbol of the wild, but in recent years they have become very accustomed to man. In some places, they are considered pests by leaving their droppings everywhere they go—walking paths, parks, golf courses and other open areas.

These are fascinating and majestic birds, and it is a shame they have sometimes received this bad rap. It is not geese's fault that the opening of the countryside into grazeable areas—good for eating, good for staying far from brush where predators might lurk—has helped them prosper.

A Canada goose is not just a Canada goose. There are several races, including the Richardson's variety—which might only be the size of a large mallard—to the interior subspecies which weighs 6 to 8 pounds to the Giant Canada goose which can weigh up to 15 pounds. Get too close to a goose of this size when it's guarding a new clutch of goslings, and you'll step aside quickly when you hear that warning "get away" hiss.

TIP: Canada geese have no qualms about living near civilization.

Canada geese feed in open country, favoring greens (such as grass, clover, alfalfa and winter wheat sprouts) as well as grains (including corn, wheat, barley and oats). A typical day would see the birds flying into a field to feed at dawn, heading back to water to spend the day, then feeding again before the sun goes down. The flocks you see in summer are usually family groups; many of these family groups will then join together for the annual spring and fall migrations.

Canada geese nest across Canada, through the top tier of states and into the central states. The birds winter across the South, but hardy birds will stay as far north as liquid water occurs, if too much snow doesn't cover the available forage.

TIP: Grains will attract geese. Spread corn, wheat, rice or other kernels on the ground.

TIP: Geese pull in winter—and spring— migrating high overhead in their "V" formations and honking to tell the world what's going on.

IDENTIFICATION

Both male and female Canada Geese have black feet, legs, tail, bill and head. The head also features a wide, white necklace/cheek patch. The back, wings and sides run a brownish gray, the breast silvery white. As described, different subspecies are different sizes, and even biologists disagree on exactly how many races there are, but the number given seems to hover around 12. As for their voice, most people are familiar with the Canada goose's strong, musical honking, which often can be heard from miles away as it carries on a spring or autumn breeze.

NESTING

A pair of Canada geese will typically mate for life, and one will take a new partner only if the other dies. The nest is a mass of plant material lined with—what else—goose down; this pile is usually placed on the ground, and near water. There the female lays 4–7 white eggs, which she incubates for 25–30 days. The goose and gander are extraordinary parents, working together to guard and protect their brood. Dominant parents seem to have the habit of adopting other geese's young, and can sometimes be seen with broods of 20 or 30 goslings. This is likely a mechanism to increase the chances of more young surviving, by placing them with the most successful parents. Half-grown geese are almost comical they are so ugly, following their parents around and waiting to fledge.

Gallery of Waterfowl

You may have opportunities to see other waterfowl in the course of birding, gardening and other outdoor activities. This gallery displays some of the ducks you might cross paths with.

Blue-Winged Teal *Anas discors*

Blue-winged teal are incredibly small for a duck (only 15 or so inches long and weighing at most a pound). They fly with great speed, darting erratically as they travel, probably as a defense against avian predators. A drake is handsome in his breeding plumage, with a blue-green speculum and a distinct white crescent on either side of his face. These ducks are dabblers. They depend heavily on rains and snowmelt filling the American heartland's pothole lakes and ponds, and in a good year almost every one will have a breeding pair of teal on it.

Green-Winged Teal *Anas crecca*

Even smaller than the blue-winged teal. The breeding drake's head is rusty red-brown, with a handsome green patch running from the eye down to the back of the neck, and a bold green speculum. Hens are mottled brown overall. Unlike other teal, greenwings are especially hardy, and are often among the last waterfowl to leave as their wetland homes freeze up in fall, and they are one of the first ducks to return in spring.

Cinnamon Teal *Anas cyanoptera*

A teal of the West. The breeding drake is especially handsome in his coat of cinnamon, with a powder-blue shoulder patch and green speculum; the bill is black, the legs and feet orange. The female cinnamon teal looks just like a female blue-wing. The marshes surrounding Utah's Great Salt Lake seem to be the center of the cinnamon teal's breeding universe, but they can be found nesting in all the other Western states as well. Cinnamon teal take off for Mexico at the first sign of frost in the fall, and don't return until spring has soothed the wetlands again.

Northern Pintail *Anas acuta*

The drake's long, pointed tail provides the name for this elegant-looking duck. A breeding male features a chocolate-brown head with a white stripe running from the neck up either side of the head. The back and sides are a detailed swirling of black and white. The hen, like other female ducks, is mottled brown; look for a bit of chocolate brown on her head. Drakes give a soft but distinctive *preep-preep* whistle; hens will quack.

Gadwall *Anas strepera*

A breeding male is subtle but lovely in his plumage of gray-barred feathers with a simple white speculum; the bill is black. A hen gadwall closely resembles a hen mallard, but lacks the colored speculum. Formerly a western duck, gadwalls now breed along the Atlantic coast as well. In some circles gadwalls are simply known as gray ducks.

American Wigeon *Anas americana*

America's bald duck, the wigeon is also called baldpate because of the breeding male's white forehead and crown. This "pate" is flanked by a deep green swath running from the eyes to the back of the head. Bold white shoulder patches show clearly while the bird is in flight, and the beak is blue-gray with a black tip. Hen wigeon are chestnut-brown; look for the beak (similar to the male's) and blue feet. Baldpates are dabblers, but like to hang out around diving ducks, often stealing the divers' catch when they emerge from a deep-water foray.

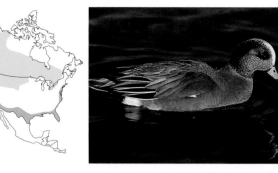

Ruddy Duck *Oxyura jamaicensis*

This chubby little diving duck is named for the ruddy chestnut color that dominates on the breeding drake. The top of the head is black, the cheeks white, and the bill an almost unbelievable baby blue. The bill turns black after breeding. The hen is dusky brown. Ruddy ducks nest across the central states, and some years it seems there's a proud male standing guard at every puddle you pass.

Lesser Scaup *Aythya affinis*

Also called bluebill. These divers feature prominent white sides, easily visible at waterline on ducks paddling the surface. The best time to see bluebills, as with most divers, is during the spring or fall migration when some birds may stop off at most any pond, lake or stream for a rest. In spring, drakes have a handsome purplish black head to go with their white sides. The hen is mottled brown, with a white patch in front of the bill. Always watch for a slaty, blue-gray bill on a duck that dives completely underwater for its food.

Greater Scaup *Aythya marila*

Very similar to the lesser scaup, but larger. A breeding male looks similar to a breeding lesser, but the head takes on a greenish tinge instead of purple. Female greaters and lessers look about the same, with a white ring encircling the bill. The usual place to see the birds is in a large grouping, far out in open water, the big white patches on their sides rolling with the waves. Greaters are also called bluebills.

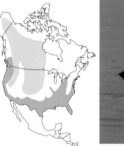

Common Goldeneye *Bucephala clangula*

Another diving duck you might notice during migration time, also called "whistler" because of the sound the flying bird's wings make. The eye is bright gold in both males and females, and the male has a greenish black head with a white spot below and in front of the eye. The back is black and the belly white, separated by black-and-white striped feathers. Hens have a brown head without the white spot, and are otherwise brown and gray.

Bufflehead *Bucephala albeola*

This small, chubby duck breeds in tree cavities, somewhat of an oddity for a member of the diving duck clan. Buffleheads stick in smaller groups than do other diving ducks, preferring to stay with their own kind. Breeding males feature a bright, white wedge behind the eye on their green-purple head; his back is black, sides and belly white. A female is dark brown and gray, and a white swatch on her cheek gives her away. "Butterball" is a common name for these round, pudgy-looking ducks.

Index